BY KENNETH PATCHEN

Selected Poems

by

Kenneth Patchen

A New Directions Paperbook

SIXTH PRINTING

The sea is awash with roses O they blow
Upon the land

The still hills fill with their scent
O the hills flow on their sweetness
As on God's hand

O love, it is so little we know of pleasure
Pleasure that lasts as the snow

But the sea is awash with roses O they blow
Upon the land

For Miriam

Do l not deal with angels
When her lips I touch

So gentle, so warm and sweet—falsity
Has no sight of her
O the world is a place of veils and roses
When she is there

l am come to her wonder
Like a boy finding a star in a haymow
And there is nothing cruel or mad or evil
Anywhere

NOTE

THE poems in this selection are taken from the following volumes and were chosen by the publisher, not the author. The provenance of each poem is listed in the table of contents by number.

CONTENTS

ix

x

xi

xii

AS SHE WAS THUS ALONE IN THE CLEAR MOON-
LIGHT, standing between rock and sky, and scarcely seem-
ing to touch the earth, her dark locks and loose garments scat-
tered by the wind, she looked like some giant spirit of the
older time, preparing to ascend into the mighty cloud which
singly hung from this poor heaven

so when she lay beside me
sleep's town went round her
and wondering children pressed against the high windows
of the room where we had been

so when she lay beside me
a voice, reminded of an old fashion:
    'What are they saying?
    of the planets and the turtles?
    of the woodsman and the bee?'
but we were too proud to answer, too tired to care about de-
      signs
    'of tents and books and swords and birds'

thus does the circle pull upon itself
and all the gadding angels draw us in

until I can join her in that soft town where the bells
split apples on their tongues
and bring sleep down like a fish's shadow.

AND WHAT WITH THE BLUNDERS, what with the
real humor of the address, the end is sure to be attained, that
of roarous fun in the roused hamlet or mountain village which
pour forth their whole population in a swarm round the

1

amorous orator, down to the baby that can but just tottle and
the curs that join in the clamor, mad with ecstasy at the nov-
elty of some noise besides that of trees and the horrible clamor
of the grass

We talked of things but all the time we wanted each other
and finally we were silent and I knelt above your body

a closing of eyes
and falling unfalteringly
over a warm pure country and something crying

when I was a child things being hurt made me sorry
for them but it seemed the way men and women did
and we had not made the world

coming into it crying
(I wanted so not to hurt you)
and going out of it like a sudden pouring of salt

later, being tired and overflowing with tenderness
girl's body to boy's body lying there and wondering what it
    had been
we got to our feet very quietly so that they would not waken
but we felt their shy sorrowful look on us as we left them alone
    there

    *   *   *   *   *

All things are one thing to the earth
rayless as a blind leper Blake lies with everyman
and the fat lord sleeps beside his bastard at last
and it doesn't matter, it doesn't mean what we think it does
for we two will never lie there
    2

*we shall not be there when death reaches out his sparkling
    hands*

there are so many little dyings that it doesn't matter which of
    them is death.

These Unreturning Destinies

The columns glow faintly
Under this comfortable moon.
In their wisdom pass
The cathedral airs of heaven.
Here night's immortal toad sings,
Its black throat puffed with mockery
Of all narrow determinations.
            Old dancers sleep
In feathery cribs, their green rhythm stilled
By the swaying of stone bells
In churches of water.
The figure of a man appears
For a moment on the steps of the temple,
Then sorrowfully withdraws to his place
In the attended shadow.
Before and around him stand
The brick and steel forests of the dead city,
And perched in the cold branches.
The birds of madness clamor.
Now is the hour of silence come.
The magnificent heads shine faintly
Upon the roads of the fish,
And are gone O they are gathered

Unto the thoughtful breast of victory.
Destiny and youth sleep in the lands
Of the walking sword.
Each one is larger than his other.
In their alternate life men hold
Untarnishing peaks.
On what man is write
Other landscapes, other fairer caverns,
Other more welcome-radiant islands
That peacefully float on his luminous waters.

The columns of death glow faintly white
Within the forests of this destroying planet.
Here gleeful beasts track each other
Through lanes of winter and rotting heroes.

Let Us Have Madness

Let us have madness openly, O men
Of my generation. Let us follow
The footsteps of this slaughtered age:
See it trail across Time's dim land
Into the closed house of eternity
With the noise that dying has,
With the face that dead things wear—

                              nor ever say

We wanted more; we looked to find
An open door, an utter deed of love,

Transforming day's evil darkness;
                    but
We found extended hell and fog
Upon the earth, and within the head
A rotting bog of lean huge graves.

We Leave You Pleasure

We leave you pleasure in the earth:
Burnt grass in the sun; waters'
Body, lovely in the waste of years,
Having no wings for us;
The stellar vast wonder in the sky; the furniture
Of Space shattered within the heart;
The cynical image of smoke curling up
From homes we never had.

We leave you seas upon parched shores;
The iron twist in vines
Over our graves: the deafening sound
Of silence over everything.
Turn from the rebel body: here;
The crude question of the grass;
The spirit's face bleary
With sightlessness. It is enough.
We leave you.

5

Do the Dead Know What Time It Is?

The old guy put down his beer.
Son, he said,
    (and a girl came over to the table where we were:
    asked us by Jack Christ to buy her a drink.)
Son, I am going to tell you something
The like of which nobody ever was told.
    (and the girl said, I've got nothing on tonight;
    how about you and me going to your place?)
I am going to tell you the story of my mother's
Meeting with God.
    (and I whispered to the girl: I don't have a room,
    but maybe. . .)
She walked up to where the top of the world is
And He came right up to her and said
So at last you've come home.
    (but maybe what?
    I thought I'd like to stay here and talk to you.)
My mother started to cry and God
Put His arms around her.
    (about what?
    Oh, just talk . . . we'll find something.)
She said it was like a fog coming over her face
And light was everywhere and a soft voice saying
You can stop crying now.
    (what can we talk about that will take all night?
    and I said that I didn't know.)
You can stop crying now.

'The Snow Is Deep on the Ground'

The snow is deep on the ground.
Always the light falls
Softly down on the hair of my belovèd.

This is a good world.
The war has failed.
God shall not forget us.
Who made the snow waits where love is.

Only a few go mad.
The sky moves in its whiteness
Like the withered hand of an old king.
God shall not forget us.
Who made the sky knows of our love.

The snow is beautiful on the ground.
And always the lights of heaven glow
Softly down on the hair of my belovèd.

The Reason for Skylarks

It was nearly morning when the giant
Reached the tree of children.
Their faces shone like white apples
On the cold dark branches
And their dresses and little coats
Made sodden gestures in the wind.

7

He did not laugh or weep or stamp
His heavy feet. He set to work at once
Lifting them tenderly down
Into a straw basket which was fixed
By a golden strap to his shoulder.
Only one did he drop—a soft pretty child
Whose hair was the color of watered milk.
She fell into the long grass
And he could not find her
Though he searched until his fingers
Bled and the full light came.

He shook his fist at the sky and called
God a bitter name.

But no answer was made and the giant
Got down on his knees before the tree
And putting his hands about the trunk
Shook
Until all the children had fallen
Into the grass. Then he pranced and stamped
Them to jelly. And still he felt no peace.
He took his half-full basket and set it afire,
Holding it by the handle until
Everything had been burned. He saw now
Two men on steaming horses approaching
From the direction of the world.
And taking a little silver flute
Out of his pocket he played tune
After tune until they came up to him.

8

She knows it's
raining and my
room is warm

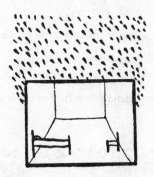

but she is proud
and beautiful
and I have
no money

9

I Feel Drunk All the Time

Jesus it's beautiful!
Great mother of big apples it is a pretty
World!

You're a bastard Mr. Death
And I wish you didn't have no look-in here.

I don't know how the rest of you feel,
But I feel drunk all the time

And I wish to hell we didn't have to die.

O you're a merry bastard Mr. Death
And I wish you didn't have no hand in this game

Because it's too damn beautiful for anybody to die.

I DON'T WANT TO STARTLE YOU but they are going to kill most of us

I knew the General only by name of course.
I said Wartface what have you done with her?
I said You Dirtylouse tell me where she is now?
His duck-eyes shifted to the Guard. All right, Sam.
I saw a photograph of the old prick's wife on the desk;
Face smiling like a bag of money on a beggar's grave.
Who is that fat turd I said—he hit me with his jewelled fist.
While his man held me he put a lighted cigarette on my eyelid.
I smelt the burning flesh through his excellent perfume.
On the wall it said *Democracy must be saved at all costs.*
The floor was littered with letters of endorsement from lib-
     erals

And intellectuals: "your high ideals," "liberty," "human jus-
    tice."
Stalin's picture spotted between Hoover's and a group-shot
    of the DAR.
I brought my knee up suddenly and caught him in the nuts.
A little foam trickled from his flabby puss. All right, Sam.
They led me into a yard and through a city of iron cells.
I saw all the boys: Lenin, Trotsky, Nin, Pierce, Rosa Luxem-
    burg. . .
Their eyes were confident, beautiful, unafraid. . . .
We came finally to an immense hall protected by barbed wire
And machineguns: Hitler, Benny Mussolini, Roosevelt and all
The big and little wigs were at table, F.D.'s arm around
    Adolf,
Chiang Kai-shek's around the Pope, all laughing fit to kill.
As soon as a treaty was signed, out the window it went;
But how they fumbled at each other under the table!
I snatched up a menu:
    Grilled Japanese Soldier On Toast
    Fried Revolutionaries à la Dirty Joe
    Roast Worker Free Style
    Hamstrung Colonial Stew, British Special
    Gassed Child's Breast, International Favorite
Wine list—Blood 1914, '15, '17, '23, '34, '36, '40 etc.
So much fresh meat I thought! A butchers' holiday. . .
The General paused to enjoy the floorshow:
On a raised platform little groups of people stood.
Flags told their nationality; orators told them what to do.
As the bands blared they rushed at each other with bayonet.
The dead and dying were dragged off and others brought on.
Sweat streamed from the orators; the musicians wobbled
    crazily.

11

The Big Shots were mad with joy, juggling in their seats like
        monkeys.
And they never get wise the General said as we moved on.
Out in the air again. . . .
A line of petty officials and war-pimps waited before the door.
As we approached they drew aside respectfully to let the
        General in.
I heard a woman moaning and I knew what they wanted there.
Now do you know what we've done with her the General said.
To go mad or to die. . .
They forced me to watch as the General went up to her and
Her eyes were looking at me.

The Rites of Darkness

The sleds of the children
Move down the right slope.
To the left, hazed in the tumbling air,
A thousand lights smudge
Within the branches of the old forest,
Like colored moons in a well of milk.

The sleds of the children
Make no sound on the hard-packed snow.
Their bright cries are not heard
On that strange hill.
The youngest are wrapped
In cloth of gold, and their scarfs
Have been dipped in blood.
All the others, from the son
Of Tegos, who is the Bishop

12

Of Black Church—near Tarn,
On to the daughter of the least slut,
Are garbed in love's shining dress;
Naked little eels, they flash
Across the amazed ice.
And behind each sled
There trots a man with his sex
Held like a whip in his snaking hand.

But no one sees the giant horse
That climbs the steps which stretch forth
Between the calling lights and that hill
Straight up to the throne of God.
He is taller than the highest tree
And his flanks steam under the cold moon.
The beat of his heart shakes the sky
And his reaching muzzle snuffles
At the most ancient star.

The innocent alone approach evil
Without fear; in their appointed flame
They acknowledge all living things.
The only evil is doubt; the only good
Is not death, but life. To be is to love.
This I thought as I stood while the snow
Fell in that bitter place, and the riders
Rode their motionless sleds into a nowhere
Of sleep. Ah, God, we can walk so easily,
Bed with women, do every business
That houses and roads are for, scratch
Our shanks and lug candles through

13

These caves; but, God, we can't believe,
We can't believe in anything.
Because nothing is pure enough.
Because nothing will ever happen
To make us good in our own sight.
Because nothing is evil enough.

I squat on my heels, raise my head
To the moon, and howl.
I dig my nails into my sides,
And laugh when the snow turns red.
As I bend to drink,
I laugh at everything that anyone loves.

All your damn horses climbing to heaven

'O Fiery River'

O fiery river
Flow out over the land.
Men have destroyed the roads of wonder,
And their cities squat like black toads
In the orchards of life.
Nothing is clean, or real, or as a girl,
Naked to love, or to be a man with.
The arts of this American land
Stink in the air of mountains;
What has made these men sick rats
That they find out every cheap hole?
14

How can these squeak of greatness?
Push your drugstore-culture into the sewer
With the rest of your creation.
The bell wasn't meant to toll for you.
Keep your filthy little hands off it.

O fiery river
Spread over this American land.
Drown out the falsity, the smug contempt
For what does not pay . . .
What would you pay Christ to die again?

The Origin of Baseball

Someone had been walking in and out
Of the world without coming
To much decision about anything.
The sun seemed too hot most of the time.
There weren't enough birds around
And the hills had a silly look
When he got on top of one.
The girls in heaven, however, thought
Nothing of asking to see his watch
Like you would want someone to tell
A joke—"Time," they'd say, "what's
That mean—time?", laughing with the edges
Of their white mouths, like a flutter of paper
In a madhouse. And he'd stumble over
General Sherman or Elizabeth B.
Browning, muttering, "Can't you keep

Your big wings out of the aisle?" But down
Again, there'd be millions of people without
Enough to eat and men with guns just
Standing there shooting each other.

So he wanted to throw something
And he picked up a baseball.

The Grand Palace of Versailles

An elephant made of cotton . . .
Towers of lace under which satin-heeled
Gentlemen sit, playing with the bustles
Of slightly desiccated Grandes Damns.
Good morning, Louis; it's a fine day
In the mirror.

A chaise longue carved
Out of the living body of a white leopard . . .
Spools of silk placed in buckets
Of gilt milk . . . A three-headed dancer
Prancing to the music of a little bell
Languidly swung by a Negro with a hairlip.
Two visiting kings having their canes reheaded,
While a painter to the court tints their eyebrows
With the juice of mildly sickening berries.
What does Salvador Ernst Matta, Louis?
It's a fine day in the mirror.

It must be amusing to be poor, n'est-ce pas?

Irkalla's White Caves

I believe that a young woman
Is standing in a circle of lions
On the other side of the sky.

In a little while I must carry her the flowers
Which only fade here; and she will not cry
If my hands are not very full.

Fiery antlers toss within the forests of heaven
And ocean's plaintive towns
Echo the tread of celestial feet.
O the beautiful eyes stare down . . .
What have we done that we are blessèd?
What have we died that we hasten to God?

And all the animals are asleep again
In their separate caves.
Hairy bellies distended with their kill.
Culture blubbering in and out
Like the breath of a stranded fish.
Crucifixion in wax. The test-tube messiahs.
Immaculate fornication under the smoking walls
Of a dead world.
                    I dig for my death
        in this thousand-watt dungheap.
            There isn't even enough clean air

To die in.

      O blood-bearded destroyer!
      In other times . . .
      (soundless barges float
      down the rivers of death)
      In another heart
These crimes may not flower . . .
What have we done that we are blessèd?
What have we damned that we are blinded?

Now, with my seven-holed head open
On the air whence comes a fabulous mariner
To take his place among the spheres—
The air which is God
And the mariner who is sleep—I fold
Upon myself like a bird over flames. Then
All my nightbound juices sing. Snails
Pop out of unexpected places and the long
      light lances of waterbulls plunge
        into the green crotch of my native land.
Eyes peer out of the seaweed that gently sways
Above the towers and salt gates of a lost world.

On the other side of the sky
A young woman is standing
In a circle of lions—
The young woman who is dream
And the lions which are death.

We Must Be Slow

For you and I are bathed in silence:
Here where the country all about
Is quiet; asleep in the softness
Of this evening star, sparkling
On the wrist of night. The village lights,
Like ancient bards at prayer, come
Gently to us over fields of growing corn
And docile sheep. We'd like belonging
Here, where sleep is not of city-kind,
Where sleep is full and light and close
As outline of a leaf in glass of tea; but
Knowledge in the heart of each of us
Has painted rotten eyes within
The head: we have no choice: we see
All weeping things and gaudy days
Upon this humble earth, blending
Taxis' horns and giant despair
With every landscape, here, or anywhere.

The Wolf of Winter

The wolf of winter
Devours roads and towns
In his white hunger.

The wolf of winter
Sticks his paw into the city's rancid pot,
Wanly stirring its soup of whores and suicides.

19

O the wolf of winter
Crunches on the bones of the poor
In his chill white cave.

The wolf of winter . . .
The grim, the cold, the white
Beautiful winter wolf
That feeds on our world.

The Billion Freedoms

Yes, then, always, as the rain, a star,
Or snow, the snow, snow,
Faces in the village, many dead on the roads
Of Europe, guns, go, yell, fall, O wait, what
Does life do, I know, knew, go mad, life goes
Mad, as the gentle rain, run, as the cold death
Comes into, into you, into the
Star-being man, is it quiet, quiet in the ground,
I grin, gunned silly, noble, is it noble to be part
Of, of the lie, it is a lie, war is, war is a lie,
What else is war, war is also a lie, love is not
A lie, love is greater, O love is greater
Than, war, wake my brothers, love is not a, lie,
Live, as the earth, as the, sun,
Stand in the beautiful, be, as the clean, full, fine,
Strong lives stood, hated, mocked, despised, drowned
In the sewers of poverty,
And in the sewers of the State, as Christ, was, for
He believed in life,

He believed in love, and in death, and war, and greed,
He did not believe, and any man who speaks
Of a Christian war, or of war as the savior
Of anything, that man is a liar, and
A, murderer, for no man can acquire position,
Or goods, or selfrighteousness
In a lie, except he be himself an enemy of truth,
And life, and God,
And a defiler in the temple of his kind, faces
In the villages of the world, millions dead
On the roads of Europe, what sin against reason
Is this, that they fought, fight, in a war
To save the evils
That cause war, for war is no evil
To those who have warred against the people,
And against truth, always, what crime
Against the soul of man is this, this fraud,
This mockery of life, that what is cheapest,
And dirtiest, and most debased, is thus smugly
Stamped on the forehead of, Christ, Who said,
Says, in the authority of God, thou shalt not
Kill, or take from another, O what are men
For, or God, now, as the light, and the good,
And the truth, and the love of one poor creature
For his fellow, fall, and the grandeur
Of mankind, like a blind snake,
Crawls, on its belly, into the slimy
Pit of oblivion, yes, then, always, as the rain,
A star, or as a fire burning forever in, all men.

Fall of the Evening Star

Speak softly; sun going down
Out of sight. Come near me now.

Dear dying fall of wings as birds
Complain against the gathering dark. . .

Exaggerate the green blood in grass;
The music of leaves scraping space;

Multiply the stillness by one sound;
By one syllable of your name. . .

And all that is little is soon giant,
All that is rare grows in common beauty

To rest with my mouth on your mouth
As somewhere a stars falls

And the earth takes it softly, in natural love. . .
Exactly as we take each other . . . and go to sleep.

The Fox

Because the snow is deep
Without spot that white falling through white air

Because she limps a little—bleeds
Where they shot her

Because hunters have guns
And dogs have hangmen's legs

Because I'd like to take her in my arms
And tend her wound

Because she can't afford to die
Killing the young in her belly

I don't know what to say of a soldier's dying
Because there are no proportions in death.

Instructions for Angels

Take the useful events
For your tall.
Red mouth.
Blue weather.
To hell with power and hate and war.

The mouth of a pretty girl . . .
The weather in the highest soul . . .
Put the tips of your fingers
On a baby man;
Teach him to be beautiful.
To hell with power and hate and war.

Tell God that we like
The rain, and snow, and flowers,
And trees, and all things gentle and clean
    23

That have growth on the earth.
White winds.
Golden fields.
To hell with power and hate and war.

A Temple

To leave the earth was my wish, and no will
stayed my rising.
Early, before the sun had filled the roads with carts
conveying folk to weddings and to murders;
before men left their selves of sleep, to wander
in the dark of the world like whipped beasts.

I took no pack. I had no horse, no staff, no gun.
I got up a little way and something called me,
saying,
"Put your hand in mine. We will seek God together."
And I answered,
"It is your father who is lost, not mine."
Then the sky filled with tears of blood, and snakes sang.

*SHE HAD CONCEALED HIM IN A DEEP DARK CAVE,
hewn far in the rock, to which she alone knew the entrance
on the world, and so treacherous and uncertain was the de-
scent that the law-givers and the villagers passed over his head
in the clear fields above, content to allow him such safety as
he had*

Going to bed
and when we have done
Lying quietly together in the dark

Warm houses stand within us
Sleepy angels smile in doorways
Little jewelled horses jolt by without sound
Everyone is rich and no one has money
I can love you Thank God I can love you
All that can happen to us is not known to the guns

    Are you awake darling?
    Do not fall asleep yet
to sleep now would seem a way to die so easily
and death is something which poems must be about

but the way our bodies were wings
flying in and out of each other. . .

The Hangman's Great Hands

And all that is this day. . .
The boy with cap slung over what had been a face. . .
Somehow the cop will sleep tonight, will make love to his
    wife. . .
Anger won't help. I was born angry.
Angry that my father was being burnt alive in the mills;
Angry that none of us knew anything but filth and poverty.
Angry because I was that very one somebody was supposed
To be fighting for
   25

Turn him over; take a good look at his face. . .
Somebody is going to see that face for a long time.

I wash his hands that in the brightness they will shine.

We have a parent called the earth.
To be these buds and trees; this tameless bird
Within the ground; this season's act upon the fields of Man.
To be equal to the littlest thing alive,
While all the swarming stars move silent through
The merest flower . . . but the fog of guns. . .
The face with all the draining future left blank. . .
Those smug saints, whether of church or Stalin,
Can get off the back of my people, and stay off.
Somebody is supposed to be fighting for somebody. . .
And Lenin is terribly silent, terribly silent and dead.

November 1937

The Forms of Knowledge

We moved down the valley
Past the stalls where the sun horses
Champed their bits of gold; and whence
Night's murmuring rivers flow
Onto the world.

Her two legs were beautiful
When we paused on the green bed
And I lifted her down. She sobbed

26

Once, then her mouth bruised mine;
Her hands turned to fire. She made
Red flowers on my neck when
I took her.
               At cloud level we ate,
The crumbs falling unheeded from our puffed lips. Below us
Stretched the unknown lands of sorrow.
Men had little wisdom there. They sat
In their filth like sick dogs, vomiting up
Their food. And they fought that nothing
Might be changed. In the image of God.

Now that we really see them, the other beings,
Our eyes are not strange.
Alive! standing just out of reach
Beyond where the dead cry.
So the challenge! So this destiny
Builds pleasure. My wish
Is gathered unto the silent breast. My gain
Is for all men. My eyes gleam steadily
Above this night.
               The other creatures
Come to taste my will. I separate the seeing
From the thing seen: my eyes
Think the new islands. I have heard
The sound of immense wings
Beating over their unshadowed hills.
Not to be separated from my world . . . O walk
At my side on these endless heights.

27

Who will? O who will harry the dark
At the side of the damned . . .

Calling to each other across the graves,
The beautiful and strong whom
Horror eats, whose bones are already
Bleached in city deserts, whose stars
And moons bestride another world—
These, these few, these *holy*—
They are not drowned by the great white rains
Of this winter; they are not trampled
By the horses of murder and death;
Instead, they try to live above life,
As the birds above their flying,
As the dead beyond their dying.

Leviathan's scales sparkle in the heavens
And the whole fish of the universe
Turns on the enraptured spit of God.
Through the flames I can see the lowered faces
Of creatures that watch us in amused love.
We live on only one side of the world.

As we moved down the valley
The petals of the snowflower
Dropped gently on all that had been ugly
Anywhere on this principal star.

The Stars Go to Sleep so Peacefully

The stars go to sleep so peacefully . . .
Their high gentle eyes closing like white flowers
In a child's dream of paradise.

With the morning, in house after grim house,
In a haste of money, proper to kiss their war,
These noble little fools awake.

O the soul of the world is dead . . .
Truth rots in a bloody ditch;
And love is impaled on a million bayonets

But great God! the stars go to sleep so peacefully

The Character of Love Seen as a
Search for the Lost

You, the woman; I, the man; this, the world:
And each is the work of all.

There is the muffled step in the snow; the stranger;
The crippled wren; the nun; the dancer; the Jesus-wing
Over the walkers in the village; and there are
Many beautiful arms about us and the things we know.

See how those stars tramp over heaven on their sticks
Of ancient light: with what simplicity that blue
Takes eternity into the quiet cave of God, where Caesar

And Socrates, like primitive paintings on a wall,
Look, with idiot eyes, on the world where we two are.

You, the sought for; I, the seeker; this, the search:
And each is the mission of all.

For greatness is only the drayhorse that coaxes
The built cart out; and where we go is reason.
But genius is an enormous littleness, a trickling
Of heart that covers alike the hare and the hunter.

How smoothly, like the sleep of a flower, love,
The grassy wind moves over night's tensé meadow:
See how the great wooden eyes of the forest
Stare upon the architecture of our innocence.

You, the village; I, the stranger; this, the road:
And each is the work of all.

Then, not that man do more, or stop pity; but that he be
Wider in living; that all his cities fly a clean flag. . .
We have been alone too long, love; it is terribly late
For the pierced feet on the water and we must not die now.

Have you wondered why all the windows in heaven were
    broken?
Have you seen the homeless in the open grave of God's hand?
Do you want to acquaint the larks with the fatuous music of
    war?

There is the muffled step in the snow; the stranger;
The crippled wren; the nun; the dancer; the Jesus-wing

Over the walkers in the village; and there are
Many desperate arms about us and the things we know.

Continuation of the Landscape

Definite motion is accomplished
Where all seems fixed in the orderly molds
Of sight (through the mastery and knowledge
    of natural signs we can renew
    ourselves with an ancient innocence):
These forests have the sanctity of the quiet tides
Rolling over their green reaching, yet
They do not improve upon their real station,
Which is to grow as it was first decreed.
The white bird and the snail vary the world
By the exact condition of their being; only man
Would change his distance from that beautiful center;
Only man, undirected and naked, would run
From the creature which inhabits his kind.

That to this dark village, unsummoned, unattended
By guide or acclaim, with more joy than sorrow,
I come; is not without its moment on the clock
Of my endeavor. Only through losing our place
    in this overlapping circle of wombs,
    can we attain to that ultimate pattern
Where childhood selects its running wing and grave.

A queen with transparent breasts is found
On the slope of the black hill.
She has a flowing and a meaning
Which the distance dims.
Shape of head distorted by three long swinging poles
That seem to batter through her skull—
Though this may be more than the lances
Of her companions, who are obscured
By the way the air is torn across in that place.
In fact, this whole scene is frayed and indistinct,
Almost as if it had been too long in the world,
And seen by no one really to make it luminous.

A man made of water and a shoulder-high heart
Are proceeding at a slow pace before.
Just behind come two pretty scintillating claws
Dressed as tavern maids, one of them
Riding on the horns of a small yellow wolf.
They are all intent on an object or ideal
Which seems to be harbored just above me.
The heart moves its head from side to side,
And in each of its eyes there is a tiny slit
Through which a cross looks.

'For Losing Her Love All Would I Profane'

For losing her love all would I profane
As a man who washes his heart in filth.
She wakes so whitely at my side,
Her two breasts like bowls of snow

32

Upon which I put my hands like players
In a child's story of heaven.

For gaining her love all would I protest
As a man who threatens God with murder.
Her lips part sleep's jewelled rain
Like little red boats on a Sunday lake.
I know nothing about men who die
Like beasts in a war-fouled ditch—
My sweetling . . .

O God what shall become of us?

'As We Are So Wonderfully Done with Each Other'

As we are so wonderfully done with each other
We can walk into our separate sleep
On floors of music where the milkwhite cloak of childhood
    lies

Oh my love, my golden lark, my soft long doll
Your lips have splashed my dull house with print of flowers
My hands are crooked where they spilled over your dear
    curving

It is good to be weary from that brilliant work
It is being God to feel your breathing under me

A waterglass on the bureau fills with morning . . .
Don't let anyone in to wake us

33

HE WAS ALONE (AS IN REALITY) UPON HIS HUM-BLE BED, when imagination brought to his ears the sound of many voices again singing the slow and monotonous psalm which was interrupted by the outcries of some unseen things who attempted to enter his chamber, and, amid yells of fear and execrations of anger, bade him "Arise and come forth and aid;" then the coffined form, which slept so quietly below, stood by his side and in beseeching accents bade him "Arise and save what is beautiful"

Come back when fog drifts out over the city
And sleep puts her kind hands on all these poor devils

Come back when the policeman is in another street
And Beatrice will let you see her thin soul under the paint

Come back to the corner and tell them, what brand of poison
    you want
Ask them why your very own dear lady is always on the lay

Somebody will pick up the pieces, somebody will put you to
    bed
You're a great guy, and she's the finest broad in all the world

Take it easy, partner, death is not such a bad chaser
And you didn't mix this one anyway

They were all right, the lot of them, it wasn't up to them
And they knew it; if somebody had come along and said
I've got a spot for a twolegged animal in the world I'm work-
    ing on,
They wouldn't have made anything like they had been made.
34

They were wise that this man-business was just a matter
Of putting it in and taking it out, and that went all the way
From throwing up cathedrals to getting hot pants over Kathy.
Maybe there was something to get steamed about, maybe it was
Baseball to grow a beard and end up on a cross so that a lot
Of hysteria cases could have something to slap around;
Maybe the old Greek boy knew what he was doing when he
    hemlocked
It out, loving the heels who hobbled him; maybe little French
    Joan
Got a kick out of the English hot-foot; the boys at the corner
    bar
Were willing to believe it. No skin off their noses. But what
    was hard
Was when you got a snoot full and all you can think to say
    starts with s
And you know damn well you're a good guy and you'll never
    meet a dame
Who really has your address, who can really dot your t

Come back when it's old home week in this particular hell
And you can bum enough nickels to take the fallen angels out

I sat down and said beer thinking Scotch and there by God
Was my woman just as I had always known she would be
And I went over to her and she said come home with me
Like that, raining a bit, will you get wet? no, let's hurry,
Climbing the stairs behind her, watching; what's your name?
Lorraine, don't make so much noise, the landlady; buzz her I
    said
Wondering how God could have gotten it all into this little
    tail;

35

Key in the lock, light; hello, you're lovely did you know that?
She was all right, all of her, it was up to me and I knew it; let's
Talk first, do you mind? I said no and she said some female
    stuff
Husband on the lam and I've never done this before tonight;
    me, I
Put all my cards on the table and dealt myself five aces, great
    God
I was wanting it then but she said some more things and started
To cry and I slammed on my coat and said you lousy bitch
    which shut
Her up and I put my key in the lock

And when it's open, when you've got it, when it's all yours,
When nobody else in all the world is where you are,
When your arms have really gone around something,
When your thighs know all the answers to all the questions,
Why is there always one bead of sweat that doesn't come
    from either of your faces?

Come back when sleep drifts out over the city
And the good God puts His hands on all these poor devils

My Generation Reading the Newspapers

We must be slow and delicate; return
the policeman's stare with some esteem,
remember this is not a shadow play
of doves and geese but this is now
the time to write it down, record the words—

I mean we should have left some pride
of youth and not forget the destiny of men
who say goodbye to the wives and homes
they've read about at breakfast in a restaurant:
"My love."—without regret or bitterness
obtain the measure of the stride we make,
the latest song has chosen a theme of love
delivering us from all evil—destroy . . . ?
why no . . . this too is fanciful . . . funny how
hard it is to be slow and delicate in this,
this thing of framing words to mark this grave
I mean nothing short of blood in every street
on earth can fitly voice the loss of these.

For the Mother of My Mother's Mother

Wind. Flower. Pretty village.
1847.

This is the autumn, Jenny.
Leaves scratch
The lowest star.
Green are the leaves, Jenny.

Pleasure in a warm young body . . .

Dogs snap
At the sullen moon.
Cruel are the dogs, Jenny.
They do their crazysad love
Over your sleeping face.
Snow. Rain. A bad world.

37

Jenny, my darling Jenny . . .
Black are the leaves that fall
On your grave.

*BEHOLD, ONE OF SEVERAL LITTLE CHRISTS, with
a curiously haunted ugly face, crouched beneath the first and
the last, embracing you in its horrible arms, blowing its fetid
breath in your face and using fearful threats of death and of
judgment*

Their war-boots said bigshots to the plank floor.
    I am the timorous mouse, brother mortal, take aim
    at my wee brown eye and you will hit William T. God.
Bring her in Leather Face said: he is my leader, a strong boy
And the dirt of many marches is on his soul; swarms of camp
        fires
In the bush-country, lions like bastard druids, telling us
To come out and give them a taste, and the dust and the sand
When the water is gone and you wonder what you are there
        for,
Not believing the stuff about flags after you have seen a man
        dance
Rope-necked on a dirty platform and the pretty girls yelling
        like mad
Moving their thighs as though Death were coming into them
        too.
    I am the crafty Caesar and my baby sister shall one day
    be whore to all the world, tastefully gowned in your guts.
Beautiful my heart said when I saw her.
She was very young and everything good was in her face.
I could have been Christ if she had touched me.
38

Nail her to the door my leader said and they put knives
Through her hands and knives through her feet, but
I did not turn my face away
    I am a singer of songs and there is no one
    listening now
Flame of all the world, honor of the wounded tiger,
There is something that has not been said,
There is something that can not be said,
To The Word which is the girl who hangs here,
To the one upon whom her eyes now are
For her pain, for her innocence, for her pigeon-mouthed death
That coos and trills over the fogsweet deeps of her flesh,
For those who killed her and for the strange planet of her
    dying,
For all the mockery of the just and for the battlements of salt
That man has against the howling dark
There is nothing, there is no voice, no quiet hand,
There is the sneer of the bat and the gull's fang,
There is a lobster beating his breast and singing,
Yea, singing, I am the answer to your prayer, sugar,
I am the one to come to your window in the first stinking
    sweat
Of night and I shall bed thee down in star-manure,
A pot of green paint for thy Jerusalem, believe me,
Babe, till the seas gang gok my rod shall comfort thee
    I am of the first thing and of the last thing
    Mine is the face in your dream
    Mine is the body beside you in the night
Why isn't she dead grumbled the leader
It was getting later than the night had room for
And the lanterns were beginning to look silly
(Birds pleading with something out in the swamp)
  39

Our faces hunched over our brains like tight pods.
We looked again at the maps and a little stream of her blood
Had made a river that we had no fit equipment to cross
And her hand had fallen over the city that we hoped to take
Her hair went over us praying here all of us not the least
Nor the greatest not the pure alone but those who are most
　　　　bent
On murder the evil more than the good over the lost and the
　　　　hunted
Over the gambler and the bitch followed by the whole human
　　　　pack

Written After Reading an Item in the Paper
About a Young Lady Who Went Mad upon
Forsaking Her Lover. He is Here Assumed
to Speak

Our chief amusement was to lie naked
In a little clearing deep within the forest.
There, while the things of fur and wing
Disported themselves about us, we lay
Together in peace and joy, our mouths
Completing what our voices could not tell.
We had no thought to enter the Anthian cave,
Which the repeated warnings of the wood folk
Had made sinister and unholy.
This was the place of love O cry cry air
Water earth fields birds and the calling
Of the wild swan O how we were taken
Into the green halls

Into the beautiful green halls where God dwelt.
This was the throne of song O fill fill her heart
Breast arms lips eyes and the falling
Of her golden hair O how I was tried
By that haunting flood
By that falling of love's swift unquenchable whips.
Within her queenly land I knew my wanton home.
Fair were the deeds of our revels, a pageantry
Of glory the acts of our two souls—we drank
The waters of fire, twisting upon a whirling sun,
And were drowned. In place of monuments
We built honor itself; and she instead of ornament
Had fashioned gowns for Beauty to wear.

The awesome houses of earth's innocents . . .

O my lords and ladies, pain walks upon my land . . .
Little snake, little snake, what a pretty pair
We make

I am thirsty! I am heavy with my stone!
That was the place of love O cry cry stars
Rain night snow death and the calling
Of the stained creature O how we were tortured
By that sublime beast
By that tongueless Horror which dwelt in the cave.
For you grew tired of our love.
Hovering in the air above heaven,
You dived down drunken with our constellations . . .
Because you grew tired of all the common mysteries,

41

Because you grew tired of love itself.
Not heeding the warnings of the wood folk,
You went into the cave. O cry cry my heart
Throat hands tongue spirit and the killing
Of my awesome house O how you were tested
By that murder
By that long murder which in killing love killed thee.
For I have nearly forgotten thy deeps;
Almost am I able to pass that mocking place
Without running a knife through my heart.
You were my only house O cry cry Horror
Be kind to her in your cave

'For Whose Adornment'

For whose adornment the mouths
Of roses open in languorous speech;
And from whose grace the trees of heaven
Learn their white standing

(I must go now to cash in the milk bottles
So I can phone somebody
For enough money for our supper.)

'Of the Same Beauty Were Stars Made'

Of the same beauty were stars made
That they might guide their earthly sister

When she undertook the white still journey
Into the country of His gentle keeping.

To a Certain Section of Our Population

It is ordered now
That you push your beliefs
Up out of the filth high enough
For the inchworm to get their measure.

May I Ask You a Question, Mr. Youngstown
Sheet & Tube?

Mean grimy houses, shades drawn
Against the yellow-brown smoke
That blows in
Every minute of every day. And
Every minute of every night. To bake a cake or have a baby,
With the taste of tar in your mouth. To wash clothes or fix
    supper,
With the taste of tar in your mouth. Ah, but the grand
    funerals . . .
Rain hitting down
On the shiny hearses. "And it's a fine man he was, such a com-
fort
To his old ma.—Struck cold in the flower of his youth." Bed-
rooms
43

Gray-dim with the rumor of old sweat and urine. Pot roasts
And boiled spuds; *Ranch Romances* and The Bleeding Heart
Of Our Dear Lord—"Be a good lad . . . run down to Tim's
And get this wee pail filled for your old father now." The kids
Come on like the green leaves in the spring, but I'm not spry
Anymore and the missus do lose the bloom from her soft
    cheek.
(And of a Saturday night then, in Tim O'Sullivan's Elite
    Tavern itself:
"It is a world of sadness we live in, Micky boy."
"Aye, that it is. And better we drink to that."
"This one more, for home is where I should be now."
"Aye, but where's the home for the soul of a man!"
"It's a frail woman ye act like, my Micky."
"And it be a dumb goose who hasn't a tear to shed this night.")

Rain dripping down from a rusty evespout
Into the gray-fat cinders of the millyard . . .
The dayshift goes on in four minutes.

The Climate of War

Therefore the constant powers do not lessen;
Nor is the property of the spirit scattered
On the cold hills of these events.
Through what is heavy into what is only light,
Man accumulates his original mastery
—Which is to be one with that gentle substance
Out of which the flowers take breath.

44

That which is given in birth
Is taken to purer beginnings.
The combats of this world
Rise only upward, since death
Is not man's creature, but God's . . .
And he can gain nothing by manipulating
That which is already hidden in himself.
The sources of nature are not concerned
In peoples, or in battlefields; nor are they mindful
Of the intensity with which man extinguishes his kind.
He who can give light to the hidden
May alone speak of victories.
He who can come to his own formulation
Shall be found to assume mastery
Over the roads which lead
On the whole human event.

The hour of love and dignity and peace
Is surely not dead.
With more splendor than these sombre lives
The gates within us
Open on the brilliant gardens of the sun.
Then do these inscrutable soldiers rise upward,
Nourished and flowering
On the battleslopes of the Unseen. For Victory,
Unlike the sponsored madness in these undertakings,
Is not diminished by what is mortal; but on its peaks
Grows until the dark caverns are alight
With the ordained radiance of all mankind.

THE IMPATIENT EXPLORER

INVENTS
A BOX IN WHICH
ALL JOURNEYS
MAY BE KEPT

Street Corner College

Next year the grave grass will cover us.
We stand now, and laugh;
Watching the girls go by;
Betting on slow horses; drinking cheap gin.
We have nothing to do; nowhere to go; nobody.

Last year was a year ago; nothing more.
We weren't younger then; nor older now.

We manage to have the look that young men have;
We feel nothing behind our faces, one way or other.

We shall probably not be quite dead when we die.
We were never anything all the way; not even soldiers.

We are the insulted, brother, the desolate boys.
Sleepwalkers in a dark and terrible land,
Where solitude is a dirty knife at our throats.
Cold stars watch us, chum
Cold stars and the whores

Credit to Paradise

The golden blood of the sun
Floods down in splendid abandon;
And what is full of dread
Dreams within the heart—for look,
We expect most from what we fear.

47

Even in this sun, which spreads its glorious
Image on our lives, is only caught
Again by the great frozen hand
Which tossed it forth. For think,
Wouldn't it be more a sun
If just once it could elude Him? If just once
It missed the relentless fingers?

The great can be little.
The fun of being God would be
In being nothing;
To really live, we should be dead too.
Isn't all our dread a dread of being
Just here? of being only this?
Of having no other thing to become?
Of having nowhere to go really
But where we are?

What power has the sun
If it must remain the sun?
We are afraid that one day the hand
Will not catch us when we come;
That the remorseless fingers will not close over us.

And I think that is our strongest will—
The reason all our dreams of paradise
Are dreams of an unlimited disorder
In a lawless anonymity.

Birthday Greetings for W. C. (hurchill) and His Pals

Beings so hideous that the air weeps blood
And the forehead of God shrivels,
Advance toward us.
Smiling, they hand Mrs. Buell a tin pail
Of soldier's livers and slayweed.

Mrs. Buell looks hopefully at Alfred.
"Tell me, dear, what are we to do now?"
"Just sit tight until the soul plasma gets here."

Lubby Stevers grins. He lifts his right leg
And squirts all over Christ.
"I am a gentleman, I am—an Imperial
Gentleman, that's me."

"Here's one we haven't killed yet," Jake Joel exclaims
Happily. "Let's pull his
You-know-what off first, though."
"Oh, goodie, goodie," cried Harry, "it'll make
Such a nice trinket for my missus."

Ah! a noble work is man . . .
Ah! a noble day for the Civilized Nations . . .

But I'd advise you to sit pretty tight
Until the soul plasma gets here.

49

The Cloth of the Tempest

These of living emanate a formidable light,
Which is equal to death, and when used
Gives increase eternally.
What fortifies in separate thought
Is not drawn by wind or by man defiled.
So whispers the parable of doubleness.
As it is necessary not to submit
To power which weakens the hidden forms;
It is extraordinarily more essential
Not to deny welcome to these originating forces
When they gather within our heat
To give us habitation.
The one life must be attempted with the other,
That we may embark upon the fiery work
For which we were certainly made.

What has been separated from the mother,
Must again be joined; for we were born of spirit,
And to spirit all mortal things return,
As it is necessary in the method of earth.
So sings the parable of singleness.
My comforter does not conceal his face;
I have seen appearances that were not marshalled
By sleep.
          Perhaps I am to be stationed
At the nets which move through this completing sea.
Or I have hunting on my sign.

Yet the ground is visible,
The center of our seeing. (The houses rest
50

Like sentinels on this hawking star.
Two women are bathing near a trestle;
Their bodies dress the world in golden birds;
The skin of their throats is a dancing flute . . .
How alter or change? How properly
Find an exact equation? What is flying
Anywhere that is more essential to our quest?
Even the lake . . . boat walking on its blue streets;
Organ of thunder muttering in the sky . . . A tiger
Standing on the edge of a plowed field . . .
What is necessary? What is inseparable to know?
The children seek silvery-pretty caves . . .
What are we to teach?)
The distance is not great
To worlds of magnificent joy or nowhere.

Have You Killed Your Man for Today?

In these hands, the cities; in my weather, the armies
Of better things than die
To the scaly music of war.

The different men, who are dead,
Had cunning; they sought green lives
In a world blacker than your world;
But you have nourished the taste of sickness
Until all other tastes are dull in your mouths;
It is only we who stand outside the steaming tents
Of hypocrisy and murder
Who are 'sick'—

51

This is the health you want.

Yours is the health of the pig which roots up
The vines that would give him food;
Ours is the sickness of the deer which is shot
Because it is the activity of hunters to shoot him.

In your hands, the cities; in my world, the marching
Of nobler feet than walk down a road
Deep with the corpses of every sane and beautiful thing.

Nice Day for a Lynching

The bloodhounds look like sad old judges
In a strange court. They point their noses
At the Negro jerking in the tight noose;
His feet spread crow-like above these
Honorable men who laugh as he chokes.

I don't know this black man.
I don't know these white men.

But I know that one of my hands
Is black, and one white. I know that
One part of me is being strangled,
While another part horribly laughs.

Until it changes,
I shall be forever killing; and be killed.

52

Fog

Rain's lovely gray daughter has lost her tall lover.
He whose mouth she knew; who was good to her.

I've heard her talk of him when the river lights
Scream 'Christ! it's lonely; Christ! it's cold.'

Heard the slug cry of her loneliness calling him
When the ship's mast points to no star in the North.

Many men have thought they were he;
Feeling her cold arms as they held death in theirs—

The woman-face in the frame of nothingness;
As the machinery of sleep turned its first wheel;

And they slept, while angels fell in colored sound
Upon the closing waters. Child and singing cradle one.

O sorrowful lady whose lover is that harbor
In a heaven where all we of longing lie, clinging together
    as it gets dark.

23rd Street Runs into Heaven

You stand near the window as lights wink
On along the street. Somewhere a trolley, taking
Shop-girls and clerks home, clatters through
This before-supper Sabbath. An alley cat cries
To find the garbage cans sealed; newsboys
Begin their murder-into-pennies round.

53

We are shut in, secure for a little, safe until
Tomorrow. You slip your dress off, roll down
Your stockings, careful against runs. Naked now,
With soft light on soft flesh, you pause
For a moment; turn and face me—
Smile in a way that only women know
Who have lain long with their lover
And are made more virginal.

Our supper is plain but we are very wonderful.

There Is One Who Watches

The heavens sway at his touch,
Dropping blue pennies
Into the hand of summer.
The ears of the lark alone hear his singing.
Those who love have his waking
When their bodies are fed.
On the edge of the world
Stands his unending house.
All who have waited in the darkness
Are there shone a flowering light.
Manifest in his pattern are the crowns of destiny,
And he has speech direct with God.
Dressed in the white hoods of his anger,
Terrible soldiers empty winter on the earth.
Beneath him the wells of hair
Cloud with the warm juice of suicides;
And the splendor of all creatures is polished

By the tinkling ghost whom men call death.
All beside him nestle the eternal Guardians,
Whose kingdom is the shading of a leaf
Or the clanging open of a grave.

Can the Harp Shoot Through Its Propellers?

And I had it neatly written
                              this is the secret
   of your earth: this is its one greener tree;
   its only deep sky
                              nicely settled—holding it
The way a lover is held; stubborn of its lack
Of shame—but, a blind man, passing
In great haste, bumped my arm and gave
My words upon the dusty wind

And I stand here silent now while all the breath
Of the damn beasts snuffs about my empty hands,
Not knowing that the fashion of my art
Could not design a submarine or bomb a city.

Eve of St. Agony or The Middleclass Was Sitting on Its Fat

Man-dirt and stomachs that the sea unloads; rockets
of quick lice crawling inland, planting their damn flags,
putting their malethings in any hole that will stand still,

yapping bloody murder while they slice off each other's heads,
spewing themselves around, priesting, whoring, lording
it over little guys, messing their pants, writing gush-notes
to their grandmas, wanting somebody to do something pronto,
wanting the good thing right now and the bad stuff for the
       other boy.
Gullet, praise God for the gut with the patented zipper;
sing loud for the lads who sell ice boxes on the burning deck.
Dear reader, gentle reader, dainty little reader, this is
the way we go round the milktrucks and seamusic, Sike's trap
       and Meg's rib,
the wobbly sparrow with two strikes on the bible, behave
Alfred, your pokus is out; I used to collect old ladies,
pickling them in brine and painting mustaches on their bellies,
later I went in for stripteasing before Save Democracy Clubs;
when the joint was raided we were all caught with our pants
       down.
But I will say this: I like butter on both sides of my bread
and my sister can rape a Hun any time she's a mind to,
or the Yellow Peril for that matter; Hector, your papa's in
       the lobby.
The old days were different; the ball scores meant something
       then,
two pill in the side pocket and two bits says so; he got up
       slow see,
shook the water out of his hair, wam, tell me that ain't a sweet
       left hand;
I told her what to do and we did it, Jesus I said, is your name
       McCoy?
Maybe it was the beer or because she was only sixteen but I
       got hoarse

56

just thinking about her; married a john who travels in cotton
    underwear.
Now you take today; I don't want it. Wessex, who was that
    with I saw you lady?
Tony gave all his dough to the church; Lizzie believed in
    feeding her own face;
and that's why you'll never meet a worm who isn't an anti-
    christ, my friend,
I mean when you get down to a brass tack you'll find some
    sucker sitting on it.
Whereas. Muckle's whip and Jessie's rod, boyo, it sure looks
    black
in the gut of this particular whale. Hilda, is that a .38 in your
    handbag?

    Ghosts in packs like dogs grinning at ghosts
    Pocketless thieves in a city that never sleeps
    Chains clank, warders curse, this world is stark mad

Hey! Fatty, don't look now but that's a Revolution breathing
    down your neck.

'There Is Nothing False in Thee'

There is nothing false in thee.
In thy heat the youngest body
Has warmth and light.
In thee the quills of the sun
Find adornment.

What does not die
Is with thee.

Thou art clothed in robes of music.
Thy voice awakens wings.

And still more with thee
Are the flowers of earth made bright.

Upon thy deeps the fiery sails
Of heaven glide.

Thou art the radiance and the joy.
Thy heart shall only fail
When all else has fallen.

What does not perish
Lives in thee.

'Rest, Heart of the Tired World'

Rest, heart of the tired world.
Hush . . . go to sleep.
Men and cities keep their cold terrible watches,
And the ocean frets at these naked lands of pain.
O hushabye . . . and go to sleep.

This red rain . . .
To breathe . . .
To weep . . .

To love where only murder has been lain . . .
To find youth, and faith, and all their quick kin,
Buried deep in talking halls of horror . . .
No.
It is that we cannot see,
That we cannot hear,
That we cannot smell,
Or taste, or feel, or think;
For surely no will in heaven or earth
Could endure what we seem to possess;
We live in the shadow of a greater shadow—
But there is the sun!
And from him man shall have life,
And he shall have redress from the crimes
Of his most brutal habitation . . .

O rest, heart of the tired world.
Hush . . . and go to sleep.
There is a beautiful work for all men to do,
And we shall at last wake into the sun.

How God Was Made

On the first day
A weed led her young to drink at Eternity
but there was only one hanging eye
that withered them with its look

on the second day
A wondrous hand fashioned a bubble
and the stars sang
His branching head awake

on the third day
His heart began to beat
and the heavens foamed along their gathering roads
where the mad and the dead would walk

on the fourth day
His ribs bent around the air
and the pillars of nothingness toppled down
to become roosts for the birds that foul dreams

on the fifth day
His body stirred upon the sun
and the fiery kingdoms raised their flags
that would be lifting over us forever

on the sixth day
His mouth breathed the first word
and all the things of wonder and pain and beauty
were made ready for the poor flesh of man

on the seventh day
His sweeping eye saw what had been done
and moved into the great, gentle face
where not even God could see its terror

60

Pastoral

The dove walks with sticky feet
Upon the green crowns of the almond tree,
Its feathers smeared over the warmth
Like honey
That drips lazily down into the shadow . . .

Anyone standing in that orchard,
So filled with peace and sleep,
Would hardly have noticed the hill
Nearby
With its three strange wooden arms
Lifted above a throng of motionless people
—Above the helmets of Pilate's soldiers
Flashing like silver teeth in the sun.

Now I Went Down to the Ringside and Little Henry Armstrong Was There

They've got some pretty horses up in the long dark mountains.
Get him, boy!

They've got some nifty riders away yonder on that big sad
    road.
Get him, boy!

They've got some tall talk off in that damn fine garden.
Get him, boy!

When you can't use your left, then let the right go.
When your arms get tired, hit him with a wing.
When you can't see very good, smell where he is.

They've got some juicy steaks in that nice sweet by-and-by.
Get him, boy!

They've got a lot of poor black lads in that crummy old jail-
    house.
Get him, boy!

O they've got a lot of clean bunks up in their big wide blue sky.
That's his number, boy!

Boxers Hit Harder When Women Are Around

The sleeping face folds down over this human country
And a battle crackles through the fat, blue air above us.

Rock-a-bye poor ladies, the world was ever cruel and
    wrong. . .
And while you sleep, be sure your sons will make a mess of
    something.

Ho! ho! my hovering leopard. Ho! my hungry dogs. . .
Inspect my savage house;
Here the moth-bladed light stabs at fake, lancing remote lies.

Do they stir in their troubled sleep?
Somebody will always look out for my poor ladies. . .
Rock-a-bye my darlings, the world won't always be wrong.

62

The sleeping face folds down over the broken harlot
Who stands behind the plough unshakeable,
Bewildered as all the bells in the world thunder
Against the castles where chained tigers await
The tread of the Huntsman from whose hand they will feed,
From whose desperate heart will flower a manflame honor.

Who fights the gunclan will wear hard gloves and come out
    fighting. . .
And it won't seem so lonesome when the lights are all on.

The Poor Child with the Hooked Hands

He leads me into much that is sorrow
For his name might have been mine

He comes like a dead thing giving
Pennies that I would place upon the eyes
Of those who live in private horror
And all the rooms in them haunted by war

He calls for a lovely woman to take him
To arms where the tired may lean as though home
Were a woman's arms about him and it never dark or lonely

Because his hands are hooked and ugly
And someone will surely want to put nails through them
As though there were any wood to hold the hell of him
Who had been a wilderness where something very beautiful
Got lost and wandered away as beautiful things always do

Death Will Amuse Them

A little girl was given a new toy
That needed no winding and would never run down
As even the best of everything will

And all day she played with it
Following happily over the floor of heaven
Until finally it rolled to the feet of God Himself

Who said: 'You must give it back now.'
Then He pointed down at two soldiers who were staring up
Hopefully

'You see, it is a very popular toy.'
And He tossed it down to them
Whose eyes would stare up in earnest when they touched it.

In Memory of Kathleen

How pitiful is her sleep.
Now her clear breath is still.
There is nothing falling tonight,
Bird or man,
As dear as she;
Nowhere that she should go
Without me. None but my calling.
Nothing but the cold cry of the snow.

How lonely does she seem.
I, who have no heaven,
Defenseless, without lands,
Must try a dream
Of the seven
Lost stars and how they put their hands
Upon her eyes that she might ever know
Nothing worse than the cold cry of snow.

The Deer and the Snake

The deer is humble, lovely as God made her
I watch her eyes and think of wonder owned

These strange priests enter the cathedral of woods
And seven Marys clean their hands to woo her

Foot lifted, dagger-sharp—her ears
Poised to their points like a leaf's head

But the snake strikes, in a velvet arc
Of murderous speed—assassin beautiful

As mountain water at which a fawn drank
Stand there, forever, while poison works

While I stand counting the arms of your Cross
Thinking that many Christs could hang there, crying.

65

Religion Is That I Love You

As time will turn our bodies straight
In single sleep, the hunger fed, heart broken
Like a bottle used by thieves

Beloved, as so late our mouths meet, leaning
Our faces close, eyes closed
Out there

        outside this window where branches toss
        in soft wind, where birds move sudden wings
Within that lame air, love, we are dying

Let us watch that sleep come, put our fingers
Through the breath falling from us

Living, we can love though dying comes near
It is its desperate singing that we must not hear

It is that we cling together, not dying near each other now

The Soldier and the Star

Rifle goes up:
Does what a rifle does.

Star is very beautiful:
Doing what a star does.
66

Tell them, O Sleeper, that some
Were slain at the start of the slaughter

Tell them, O Sleeper, that sleet and rain
Are falling on those poor riderless heads

Tell them, O Sleeper, that pitiful hands float on the water. . .
Hands that shall reach icily into their warm beds.

The State of the Nation

Understand that they were sitting just inside the door
At a little table with two full beers and two empties.
There were a few dozen people moving around, killing
Time and getting tight because nothing meant anything
Anymore
Somebody looked at a girl and somebody said
        Great things doing in Spain
But she didn't even look up, not so much as half an eye.
Then Jack picked up his beer and Nellie her beer
And their legs ground together under the table.
Somebody looked at the clock and somebody said
        Great things doing in Russia
A cop and two whores came in and he bought only two drinks
Because one of them had syphilis

No one knew just why it happened or whether
It would happen ever again on this fretful earth
But Jack picked up his beer again and Nellie her beer again
And, as though at signal, a little man hurried in,
Crossed to the bar and said Hello Steve to the barkeeper.

67

All the Bright Foam of Talk

Followed by garrulous hunters, the soft children grovel
Down the valley of sleep . . . so gentle . . . shining . . . but
Not singing
Never singing . . . it is the midnight of sense . . . mind's
Desolate cave

The decayed clock booms out in puffs of sound
That stagger like drunken apes through the streets,
Fingering the paint-stripped houses and the wood
Where death has flung all things beautiful

Watch the fantastic eyelid of that lark
How enormously lovely . . . hooded like an invisible engine
    and pulling earth's lustful plow right through the lark

The children do not remember the slow step of the mules
As they descended the hills lost in the snow
Knowing that there was no room in the inn
Where death has flung all things beautiful

There is laggard talk on the islands
Clatter of spoons as people stuff their bones
Mating in the slums and cheap movies
Fine hands folded over the tin cross where man tosses

There is no track before me, no light in the inn
At all . . . no fiery map nor singing . . . I cannot join the
    past
Who can never see as the lark does and think even in sleep

*BUT THE IMAGES OF HIS FORMER DREAMS STILL
HAUNTED HIM, and their hideous phantoms were more
powerfully renewed: again he heard the awful singing of
death, but unsung by mortals, being pealed through earth up
to the high heaven by throngs of the viewless and the mighty:
again he heard the wailing of the millions for some remem-
bered sin, and the wrath and the hatred of a world was rush-
ing in on him*

Hasten to your own gun, to your own star, to your own tribe,
Hurry while the light lasts, while still you need someone;
I don't trust this quiet, I don't like that grave over there.

Is it only death that bothers you?
So many have done it, brother.
So many have turned up their poor toes.

Is it only war that blackens you?
So many have gone there, brother.
So many have taken that boney grin.

Is it only blood that sickens you?
So many have bathed in it, brother.
So many are standing knee-deep there now.

Is it only God that heartens you?
So many have gone blind, brother.
So many have put their eyes in His cunning hock.

Is it only Man that frightens you?
So many have been fooled, brother.
So many hold that key, and that beautiful lock.

Hasten to your own kind, to your own dream, to your own
    land;
Hurry while there is still someone to go with you there . . .

THE FIGURE MOTIONED WITH ITS MANGLED HAND TOWARDS THE WALL BEHIND IT, *and uttered a melancholy cry*

It was rumored on the block
Ethel is going to let go tonight.
I made big about it, strutting
Down 5th eyeing the babies over,
Thinking they look like mudhens
Next to my little piece of tail.
She was hard to get. Her old lady
Was saving her for dough, but hell
I had class, want the moon, kid?
And I'd give it to her. Funny thing
Though, this is all a lie, I never
So much as touched her hand, she
Thinks I'm dirt, nobody else ever
Always got the wrong end of the stick.
I'd carry the mail for you, Ethel,
Stop running around with that pup,
He's got a car, sure, and jack to throw
Like water but what does he want?
What do they all want? something easy,
Something that somebody else worked for.
Ethel, lay off rich kids, you'll end dirty.

Join the world and see the army
The slime is quiet tonight, along the Jersey coast

70

The chippies discuss Democracy in awed tones
Breathes there a heel with man so dead . . .
Shoot the liquid fire to Johnnie, boy
With every rendezvous-with-death we are giving away
An autographed photo of J. P. Morgan taken in the frontline
*   trenches*

They took him down stone steps
To a cellar thick with rats.
The guard gave him a cigarette
And slapped it out of his mouth.
Moral. Don't ever knock off a cop.
Ethel, looking like a movie queen,
Descended on his cell in a mink coat.
When they fitted the black cap over his head
He knew that he'd never have another chance to be president.

AVARICE AND AMBITION ONLY WERE THE FIRST
BUILDERS OF TOWNS AND FOUNDERS OF EMPIRE;
They said, go to, let us build us a city and a tower whose top
may reach unto Heaven, and let us make us a name, lest we be
scattered abroad upon the face of the earth (Genesis XI: 4).
What was the beginning of this city? What was it but a con-
course of thieves, and a sanctuary of criminals? It was justly
named by the augury of no less than twelve vultures, and the
founder cemented his walls with the steaming blood of his
only brother. Not unlike to this was the beginning even of the
first town in the world, and such is the original sin of most
cities: Their actual increase daily with their age and growth;
the more people, the more wicked all of them; everyone
brings in his part to inflame the contagion, which becomes at
last so universal and so strong, that no precepts can be suffi-
71

cient preservatives, nor anything secure our safety, but flight
from among the infected. To spread our own disease

They scatter me from church to gutter.
They smear their doings over my hands.
I am lifted out of wombs
And never put back anywhere . . .
I look up from the grass and down from the cathedral.
They honor me with the stuff of dogs.
They place my body down and fill themselves.
I smile from the confessional and frown on the battlemount.
They offer me their wives
And kill my firstborn . . .
I am grown in their hovels like a vegetable that can be eaten.

They won't wash off my dirt.
They put me in parades and distribute pieces of my corpse.
They honor me with statues and seal me in the hardening
    mold.
I could never build a man
And I have come here to worship . . .

I have only this one wreath.
There is only one grave anywhere.

I am standing open.
You must not lower your eyes.

I want them all to know me.
I want my breath to go over them.
They should withhold nothing from me.
I am a respecter of dirt.
This is your house, you say. Then show
Yourself! I have not been on earth
Long enough to know about you. This

Collection of ills and organs means nothing
To me. Everybody gets a whack at them.
Tell me what you do inside there. I want
All your pain. I want to walk around where
You are. There is no war between us.

And every now and again somebody sneaks up and
Boots the hell out of you
But I could never build one of these curious things
And I have come here because of that simplicity

Is it so very dark in there, brothers?
Does it hurt all the time?
Does it rain without any end at all?
Are the same monsters in your streets?
Why have you nailed up your doors, brothers?
And every now and again something looks down and
Smears the doings of God over our murderous hands

I should like to pray now if I can stay out of a trench to do it
There is no war between us, brothers.
There is only one war anywhere.

'Be Music, Night'

Be music, night,
That her sleep may go
Where angels have their pale tall choirs

Be a hand, sea,
That her dreams may watch
Thy guidesman touching the green flesh of the world

Be a voice, sky,
That her beauties may be counted
And the stars will tilt their quiet faces
Into the mirror of her loveliness

Be a road, earth,
That her walking may take thee
Where the towns of heaven lift their breathing spires

O be a world and a throne, God,
That her living may find its weather
And the souls of ancient bells in a child's book
Shall lead her into Thy wondrous house

What Is the Beautiful?

The narrowing line.
Walking on the burning ground.
The ledges of stone.

74

Owlfish wading near the horizon.
Unrest in the outer districts.

Pause.

And begin again.
Needles through the eye.
Bodies cracked open like nuts.
Must have a place.
Dog has a place.

Pause.

And begin again.
Tents in the sultry weather.
Rifles hate holds.
Who is right?
Was Christ?
Is it wrong to love all men?

Pause.

And begin again.
Contagion of murder.
But the small whip hits back.
This is my life, Caesar.
I think it is good to live.

Pause.

And begin again.
Perhaps the shapes will open.

Will flying fly?
Will singing have a song?
Will the shapes of evil fall?
Will the lives of men grow clean?
Will the power be for good?
Will the power of man find its sun?
Will the power of man flame as a sun?
Will the power of man turn against death?
Who is right?
Is war?

Pause.

And begin again.
A narrow line.
Walking on the beautiful ground.
A ledge of fire.
It would take little to be free.
That no man hate another man,
Because he is black;
Because he is yellow;
Because he is white;
Or because he is English;
Or German;
Or rich;
Or poor;
Because we are everyman.

Pause.

And begin again.
It would take little to be free.

That no man live at the expense of another.
Because no man can own what belongs to all.
Because no man can kill what all must use.
Because no man can lie when all are betrayed.
Because no man can hate when all are hated.

And begin again.
I know that the shapes will open.
Flying will fly, and singing will sing.
Because the only power of man is in good.
And all evil shall fail.
Because evil does not work,
Because the white man and the black man,
The Englishman and the German,
Are not real things.
They are only pictures of things.
Their shapes, like the shapes of the tree
And the flower, have no lives in names or signs;
They are their lives, and the real is in them.
And what is real shall have life always.

Pause.

I believe in the truth.
I believe that every good thought I have,
All men shall have.
I believe that what is best in me,
Shall be found in every man.
I believe that only the beautiful
Shall survive on the earth.

I believe that the perfect shape of everything
Has been prepared;
77

And, that we do not fit our own
Is of little consequence.
Man beckons to man on this terrible road.
I believe that we are going into the darkness now;
Hundreds of years will pass before the light
Shines over the world of all men . . .
And I am blinded by its splendor.

Pause.

And begin again

The Dimensions of the Morning

Furtively sounding
In the high
Halls of God, the voice which is
Life begins to sing.
You will listen O you will not be afraid
To listen . . .
All these do:
The wolf, the fengy, the bear, the wide
Fish; and the deer, the silky rat, the snail,
The onises—even the goat
That waves his funny tail at trains
Is listening.
Do you now faintly
Hear the voice of life?
I will allow you respect for
Red apples and countries warm

78

With the races of men; peep over
The transom at China if you like;
But I will have no hatred or fear
Entering this poem.

It is big
Inside a man.
It is soft and beautiful
In him.
Water and the lands of the earth
Meet there.
I hand you a mountain.
I take the word Europe
Or the word death
And tear them into tiny pieces;
I scatter them at your feet.

Hand me a star.
Take me to a new city.
You are wasting your lives.
You are going along with your pockets
Full of trash.
You have been taught to want only the ugly
And the small;
You have been taught to hate what is clean
And of the star.
A dog will throw up
When he is sick;
Are you lower than dogs
That you keep it all down—
And cram more in?

The voice which is life
Shall sound over all the earth,
And over all who lie deep
In its green arms—
Go you to lie there as a fool, or as a child,
Tired from his beautiful playing,
To fall happily asleep?

"And When Freedom Is Achieved . . ."

You have used a word
Which means nothing.
You have given a word
The power to send men to death.
Men are not free who are sent to die.
Only those who send them are 'free.'
You should have freedom stuffed down your fat throats.

The Unfulfilling Brightnesses

Thy servant I am
Immortal are thy lion-drunk deeps

As a flower thinks
So am I one with thee

Thou art my acquaintance
In the unlevel light

80

I am falling to sleep
In thy slaying forms

Where goeth the white wind
I have been
And believe

Mohammed

And to the kings of the world,
My greeting . . .
The Kaaba shall be thrown into the sea.

These are the dusty little streets of Medina.
Here my people live.
They are poor;
But riches wait in the One True God.
All men are one man in His wisdom.

My wives have soft breasts.
Their hair smells of my sweat.
I place my hands upon their eyes
And they know my hands; what
Is kind in them, what blackened
By my greed and cunning. For
I am a man of thirsts and hungers.

And to the great of the world,
My greeting . . .
The temples of God glow through the night.

81

HOW TO BE AN ARMY

 MANY SHOES POTATOES FLAGS & FLEAS

 RIFLES TRENCHES DETERMINATION

〉〉〉〉〉〉〉〉〉〉〉〉〉〉〉〉〉〉〉〉
KNOWLEDGE OF MARCHING

$$\frac{58207}{27850} = \textbf{BLOOD}$$

+ (GENERALS)

AND A FAITH IN THE RIGHT

† †
† †
† †
† †
† †
† †

82

Gautama in the Deer Park at Benares

In a hut of mud and fire
Sits this single man—"Not to want
Money, to want a life in the world,
To want no trinkets on my name"—
And he was rich; his life lives where
Death cannot go; his honor stares
At the sun.

The fawn sleeps. The little winds
Ruffle the earth's green hair. It is
Wonderful to live. My sword rusts
In the pleasant rain. I shall not think
Anymore. I touch the face of my friend;
He shows his dirty teeth as he scratches
At a flea—and we grin. It is warm
And the rice stirs usefully in our bellies.

The fawn raises its head—the sun floods
Its soft eye with the kingdoms of life—
I think we should all go to sleep now,
And not care anymore.

The Man with the Golden Adam's Apple

There were four crates of chickens
Hanging from the topmost bough
Of an elm tree near the fairgrounds;
A Mack truck with a badly damaged fender

Was just pulling to a stop across the road,
When a lightly-clad old lady, her shawl
Draped like a tired wing, and with hip-boots
Of bright yellow fur on her shrivelled-up legs,
Suddenly transformed herself into a shepherd boy,
And went crazy-running off over the horizon.
At that precise moment a door opened in the sky,
And the man with the golden adam's apple
Stepped briskly down.

The driver of the Mack backed into a turnoff,
Gunned her up so hard she blew the muffler,
And then slouched limp at the big wheel,
A tiny black hole appearing 'as if by magic'
In the middle of his forehead.
T m w t g a a holstered his deadly automatic,
Swore softly, and taking out a purple bandana,
Removed something from the crown of his Homberg.
He did not even then look up at the chickens;
Instead, being a fellow with a keen sense of proportion,
And mindful ever of his responsibility to society,
He built a fire and set up light-housekeeping in it.

'O My Darling Troubles Heaven with her
Loveliness'

O my darling troubles heaven
With her loveliness

She is made of such cloth
That the angels cry to see her

Little gods dwell where she moves
And their hands open golden boxes
For me to lie in

She is built of lilies and candy doves
And the youngest star wakens in her hair

She calls me with the music of silver bells
And at night we step into other worlds
Like birds flying through the red and yellow air
Of childhood

O she touches me with the tips of wonder
And the angels cuddle like sleepy kittens
At our side

The Lions of Fire Shall Have Their Hunting

The lions of fire
Shall have their hunting in this black land

Their teeth shall tear at your soft throats
Their claws kill

O the lions of fire shall awake
And the valleys steam with their fury

85

Because you are sick with the dirt of your money
Because you are pigs rooting in the swill of your war
Because you are mean and sly and full of the pus of your
    pious murder
Because you have turned your faces from God
Because you have spread your filth everywhere

O the lions of fire
Wait in the crawling shadows of your world
And their terrible eyes are watching you

A Vision for the People of America

The poets with death on their tongues
shall come to address you.

The fat nonsense will end.
You will drown in your rot.

The poets with death on their tongues
shall come to address you.

The slimy hypocrisy will end.
You will go down in your filth.

O the poets with death on their tongues
shall come to address you.

The Murder of Two Men by a Young Kid Wearing Lemon-colored Gloves

                    Wait.

                                Wait.

                        Wait.

                Wait. Wait.

            Wait.

                                    Wait.

                    W a i t .

            Wait.

                        Wait.

                                Wait.

                Wait.

                            Wait.

            Wait.

                    NOW.

Red Wine and Yellow Hair

Ah that the world could use a dream or a flame cold
Teeth in their fat throats! O the lock is crusted over
With frauds and tricks, a silt of greed and compromise
O break the damn thing! And I sleep here away
From sorrow. The winding-sheet and the paler thighs
A Grecian virgin, my silken braids all tangled with night.
Is late so soon that it runs the stag and the bell to cover
Before the warm mouth can be flowered in youth's merry
        weather?
O let them remember me, and forget the lies and the hating
For the dark sex that coveteth all shall soon be their lover.
Sword on the wind, black knuckles of a thief, is this
King to be left here like a cast-off dog? the bloated
Tongues of flies licking the juice of His saving wounds?
O come a little way in, death, my lads have no supper
And the old woman she wails like a goose, ah there's plenty
Of fodder and beer as well though the bastards don't want
        a meatless
Nose like me poking round their slops. O Rosalind
And Penelope, what lovely grub they must have had!
Ragged sacks for a fool to put his neighbor in, the digging
Grave is proof that none is given what all would have.
Blather dung and rubble, a coat and sup, their meanness
Is my lot. Back down and hold your clutching gab.
Swine hiss amongst their gems and Ledas bite their nails
Above the mirrored waters of this destroying world.
O none save the fiery hunter would stay to mourn the tiger.
Dotellers told in the black dice of their cities. And I lie here
Removed from all sorrow. A withered heart and a rusted
        dagger

The Laird of Emmet, my powerful hands they squeeze at the
        dust.
Is life the meat that swings the falcon down from his highs?
Yes, a poisoned bait in the trap of a vicious fancier.
O let him chase me now, and give this slowness haste
For the dark peace that abideth here is filled with eyes.
If Fannin's river whispers the fate of my tried love
And a red wild voice laments where all sorrow lies
O Willie brought me ribbons, I thought he was so mild
Prettied me for an angel, but under a devil I got my child.
Cold rain on the talking stone, the weeping mind
Poor guest at a poorer feast, O who is born dies
And a grim hand colors the rose. O wondrous Light
Titanic wings of fire sweeping down through the night.
There was never money enough, ach I'm tired
Of showing them pictures of plump-bottomed queens
And reading aloud at wine-and-biscuity tales
Where ghosts rattle the lids of tombs and flick up like beans.
O resurrect my sons, Lord, from this empty table!
Worms begin lower, and they gather all, but the mold
Out-thinks the stone and the hangman's tree. Words of the
        flesh
Bleed out of the moving dark . . . We fall we thirst we are
        cold
While in the summer meadow lovers find what is warm.

   A broken cup and a wisp of rotted hair
Come cry come in wrath of love and be not comforted
Until the grave that is this world is torn asunder
For human the lock and human the key
O everything that lives is holy!
And Man and God are one in that mystery.

The New Being

They'd make you believe that your problem is one of sex,
That men and women have mysteriously become
Strange and fearful to one another—sick, diseased, cold—
And that is true. But no loss of a father-image or of
Any other image, did this. Why don't you face the truth for
    once?
You have accepted the whole filthy, murderous swindle with-
    out
A word of protest, hated whomever you were told to hate,
Slaughtered whomever you were told to slaughter; you've
    lied,
Cheated, made the earth stink with your very presence—
    Why
Shouldn't you despise and hate one another? Why shouldn't
Your flesh crawl everytime you touch one another?
Why should you expect to make 'love' in a bed fouled with
    corpses?

Oh, you poor, weak little frauds, sucking around
Frantically for something to ease your guilt—
Why don't you face it?
Your birthright, liferight,
Deathright, and now your
Sexright, you've lost. What
Did you expect? How
Else could it be? You've
Made property and money your only gods—
Well, this is their rule,
This is what you wanted.
And now they'll wipe you out.

Why don't you face it?
Stop sucking around.
Your pet witch-doctors can't help you,
They're all sick from the same thing.
Your pompous intellectuals can't help you,
They're all sick from the same thing.
Your sly, vicious statesmen can't help you,
They're all sick from the same thing.
Why don't you face it?

No, your problem is not one of sex—
Your problem is that you have betrayed your animal
Into hands as cruel and bloody as your own.
Man is dead.
I don't know what kind of thing you are.

A Plate of Steaming Fish

The Scene: A Fishermen's Boarding House
The Time: Many Years Ago
Menu: Choice of gudgeon, remora, tautog, skopjack,
burgall, gurnard, chogset, etc., etc.
The Speaker: A Sailor's Widow

As you would know, having lived in trouble here at my side
    For such an outwardly-long time,
I dread this hour, now, at the day's end, when seamen supper.
Sitting before this checkered cloth, the worn silk of my gown
Rubbed by their tarry legs, the thick sweat of them like a
        breathing

On my face and breasts—O tonight again, and on again for-
ever,
Listening to the shameful jokes that are meant to taunt me,
Digging my nails into the ugly tan and blue of these squares.
O come and take me back to my own people!

The flowering tree we planted outside the kitchen window is
gone.
Your brothers chopped it down and burned it.
Now I see their fyke nets and brush-hinged weirs a-drying
there.
And along the wren-gray, friendly wall,
Where I set such tiny yellow roses,
Their stabbing hooks and evil-looking lobster-cages hang.
O come and take me away from here!

And all I went to the lone cliffs, to the streaming rocks where
the sea
And the whole bitter world cried with your name—
O heart, my heart, how should I not have found thee there?
How was I to know that I lay with strangers in the rain there?
Bald Tom and Ernie Willis, Old Roaren and Captain Dona-
hue—
O mine is only a spiritual fault, my love . . .
Yet they threw me down, it was you lying above me there.
O come and make me pure again!

On the morning *The Kalinn* sailed, and its masts and spars like
the hands
Of a child waving back to us—to your mother, who is dead
now;
And to your wife, who'd rather be, than like I am,
92

This woman of forty-one, no longer straight, her skin and hair
Dried by sun and wind, and her breasts by lonely grief in the
          night—
    O as it went down in the toppling sparkle,
    And the little flowers of phosphorous
    Rested for a moment in that gray and gentle cradle,
I saw the figure of our love standing there on the water!
    And so, confused and mocked by all of them,
I wait at the side of our watching son and daughter.
    O come and take us away from here!
O rise up out of thy cold grave, Lennie
          and take us away from here . . .

The Lute in the Attic

                    As this comes in
                    Call you
I call you
The apples are red again in Chandler's Valley
        redder for what happened there
And the ducks move like flocculent clocks
        round and round, and round
The seven fat ducks whose mouths
        were wet crimson once
                O William Brewster Hollins
        I call you back!
    Come you and stand here
By the fog-blunted house that is silent now
And watch these terrible ducks moving
        slowly round the rock of Santa Maura.
    93

Your father's gone daft, Willy.
        Did you know that?
And Isalina's flaxen hair is the color of the mud
        at the bottom of Rathbeggin Creek.
Her teeth are crooked and yellow,
                more like an old, sickly dog's
        than a woman's—but her eyes
        still hold their light, people say.
(Though for me it's a very strange light, Willy.
I remember I saw a different thing there
                a few hours before it happened—
        and the two of you lying naked together
        under the apple trees.
For myself, to be truthful, her eyes have changed.
        They are not at all as they were then.)

        In his poor unease your father
Has come to love rather fearful things.
"Don't hurt my spider-ladies!" he screams
When Beth or Danny go in to clean around him.
It would be better if he died, the town whispers.

Sam Hanner drowned two summers ago.
        Old Krairly wanted to carve
'Lived on strong drink, but his last was weak'
On the stone—the Fathers said no, of course.
There was talk that Sam watched you do it.
        Did you know that?

        As this comes in
        and so much hate will go anywhere
I call you back
        94

To lie here in the rain and the dark beside the willows
Hearing the voices of lovers under the flowery hedge
              O William Brewster Hollins
I call you back!
Come you and lie here at the side of your brother . . .
    I can tell you exactly how many times
    these seven lean ducks have gone
    fiercely round the rock of Santa Maura—
And show you worse things than your father sees
And show you things far worse than your father sees, Willy.

The Orange Bears

The orange bears with soft friendly eyes
Who played with me when I was ten,
Christ, before I left home they'd had
Their paws smashed in the rolls, their backs
Seared by hot slag, their soft trusting
Bellies kicked in, their tongues ripped
Out, and I went down through the woods
To the smelly crick with Whitman
In the Haldeman-Julius edition,
And I just sat there worrying my thumbnail
Into the cover—What did he know about
Orange bears with their coats all stunk up with soft coal
And the National Guard coming over
From Wheeling to stand in front of the millgates
With drawn bayonets jeering at the strikers?

I remember you could put daisies
On the windowsill at night and in
   95

The morning they'd be so covered with soot
You couldn't tell what they were anymore.

A hell of a fat chance my orange bears had!

If a Poem Can Be Headed into Its Proper Current Someone Will Take It within His Heart to the Power and Beauty of Everybody

Arrive to arrive and to arrive here in such thick
White silence
The eye turned away
Without vanity or desire
And seeing is seen
And the music of the silence flows on the world
With a rhythm and a pulse which are changed
In the blood-beat as the heart's course by death

And hearing is heard as in the very sea
There is no sound
So in the purest thought
When vanity and desire of all mortal ends
Have been submerged
We may join the thinking which is eternally around us
And be thought about
For the common good
Of the one creature which everything is

Man is not to direct or to be directed
Anymore than a tree or a cloud or a stone

Man is not to rule or to be ruled
Anymore than a faith or a truth or a love

Man is not to doubt or to be doubted
Anymore than a wave or a seed or a fire

There is no problem in living
Which life hasn't answered to its own need

And we cannot direct, rule, or doubt what is beyond
Our highest ability to understand
We can only be humble before it
We can only worship ourselves because we are part of it

The eye in the leaf is watching out of our fingers
The ear in the stone is listening through our voices
The thought of the wave is thinking in our dreams
The faith of the seed is building with our deaths

I speak of the music of the silence
As being what is left when the singers and the dancers
Have grown still
Something is left there
A part of the reverence and of the need
A part of the fear and the pain and the wonder
And it goes on there
Coming from where it came from (O beautiful goddess!)
And reaching for what it can have little awareness of
A rhythm quite unlike any we know here
Bound and swayed as we are by the blood's orchestration
Bound and swayed as we are by the orchestration within us
By the deceptive orchestration of the blood

97

And I speak of the goddess
I speak of the goddess
I speak of the beautiful goddess

O tell them what I would say

'Do Me That Love'

Do me that love
As a tree, tree
Where birds and wind
Sing though they know
How real night is
And no one can
Go on for long
In any way
Do me that love

Do me that love
As the rain, rain
That has voices
In it, the greats'
And fools', poor dead
From old weathers—
Lives considered
And rejected
As ours will be.
The rain comes down
And flowers grow
On the graves of
98

Our enemies
Do me that love

Fog Over the Sea and the Sun Going Down

Shrouded maidens sleep on the wave,
Their garments flecked by the wounded sun—
Listen . . . (O *Nellie Malone*, only the wan silence now)
The bru-hooned Ladies are singing
Down in their cold, moving grave—
And in Captain Swaggle's skull two gwerps
Are blindly kissing.
        (O *Alba-Maria*, only the black silence now)
Sing correlay and lift the startled goddess up!
On the shore,
            as though a mouth had rested there,
            the glistening wonder!
        And floating in across the water,
These strands of gray, wet hair. . .

        Blood on the ancient water
        and darkness falling on the world.
Down the beach
The Marsden kids are torturing a snail
With a jagged stick.
(O star-led Caravans . . . "Master, Master, I fear
            this huge and surly fish!")
        Sing correlay and correlemus
For all ladies, kids, and captains
                            who're soon lost in
These coils of wet, gray hair.

99

A Pile of Rusty Beer Cans

                    If in the grave here
                    I had that other power
My rough hands on a woman's softness
Ah as it was then but no talking knows
For the one or the other a man has
Either his life or his rot anymore than
The old beer on the sleeve of a whore
Pray God tonight I am alone now and cold
Who plunged like a bull in a warm bed once
Lie here very still without plans at all
But if I knew that power moves bodies up
I would go back to her side and them fall
Weeping to be in to see us

And Hailey I'd pluck by one nude skinny leg
His lower hairs a-sweat as mine used to be
All the pale little dog of him landed
On the cans under the bedroom window
His beam-end blinking up like a twin
To that moon watched the dirt in on me

Then I would get my money from the drawer
Where she keeps her prayerbooks and teeth
And buy me a quart and a fair young miss
To get up the taste of what's down here

100

Poor Gorrel

For a woman named Gorrel
To be afraid of birds
Is neither unusual
Nor important—with other things
Like they are.

She'd never married, but
For twenty-eight years
Had the evening habit of taking
Her cats, Tom and Matilda,
With her to call on a barber
Who had a shack deep in the woods
When
And where
The four of them would munch peppermints
Until all hours.

Two weeks ago—it was raining—
Gorrel and her cats
Were hurrying home—the rain coming
Down harder and harder—when just at the old foot-bridge
—Which the rain had washed some slimy-looking grubs
On—a huge, furry owl with razor-sharp claws
Got Gorrel down and
Above the slashing sound
Of the rain a peppermint-scented scream
Rang out. The eight cats (and no wonder
Really) all had severe colds when found.

101

For Miriam

As beautiful as the hands
Of a winter tree
And as holy
Base are they beside thee

As dross beside thee

O green birds
That sing the earth to wakefulness
As tides the sea
Drab are they beside thee

As tinsel beside thee

O pure
And fair as the clouds
Wandering
Over a summer field
They are crass beside thee
The hands
Move through the starhair

As tawdry beside thee

102

Beautiful You Are

Cathedral evening, tinkle of candles
On the frosted air
Beautiful you are
Beautiful your eyes, lips, hair

Ah still they come

Evenings like chalices
Where little roofs and trees drink
Until a rude hand
Shatters them, one by one

O beautiful you are

My own
Land of holiness, unblemished grace
Springtime
In this winter place
O in the candles there
More beautiful
Than any legend's face

Your eyes, your hair

What There Is

In this my green world
Flowers birds are hands
They hold me
I am loved all day

All this pleases me

I am amused
I have to laugh from crying
Trees mountains are arms
I am loved all day

Children grass are tears

I cry
I am loved all day
Everything
Pompous makes me laugh
I am amused often enough
In this
My beautiful green world

There's love all day

All Is Safe . . .

Flow, water, the blue water
Little birds of foam
Singing on thee
O flow, water, blue water

Little stars falling asleep

To thy tossing
O flow, water, the blue water
What matters any sorrow
It is lost in thee

Little times, little men

What matters
They are safe in thee
O
Flow, water, blue water
All is safe in thee
Little birds
The shadows of maidens

Safe in thy singing

105

Lonesome Boy Blues

Oh nobody's a long time
Nowhere's a big pocket
To put little
Pieces of nice things that

Have never really happened

To anyone except
Those people who were lucky enough
Not to get born
Oh lonesome's a bad place

To get crowded into

With only
Yourself riding back and forth
On
A blind white horse
Along an empty road meeting
All your
Pals face to face

Nobody's a long time

But of Life?

What I want in heart
—*O stiller, wider, nearer*—
Said the tree
Is that none come touching

For their own stuff

Any part of
Me. And over him a wall
Of shifting fog began
To build, little on little—

Like a wet shroud.

No birds
Came then. And with them
Stars
Stayed. His poor branches
Trailed white and still. He
Wept. His
Loudest cry went unheard

So was Crucifixion's tree

The Unanswering Correspondences

Intensification of compassion; extraordinary; incalculable;
Grandeur hurls us down:
Tears blind us.
Sparrows! lions! crags! meadows! seas!

Inexhaustible; wounding; unimaginable; illimitable;

This imperishable grandeur!
The heart breaks—tears blind us—
Immensurable; unfathomable; implacable; unsayable;
We cry our animal grief—

Compassion blinds our eyes—

Each blade
Of grass, leaf of tree,
Each
Feather floating to earth,
Is a signature of love
And sorrow.
O sparrows, lions and

Seas! tears blind us.

Limpidity of Silences

In a limpidity of silences
Speaks what is unanswerable
And is answered.
In a limpidity of silences

The laurelled heads turn

Away from death
And away from life and all
Other trivial little dissolutions.
In a limpidity of silences

Sleep the laurelled heads.

The silences
Speak around us forever; yet
None
Knows what is said.
In a limpidity of silences
Reality speaks . . .
Perhaps of a maskshroud

Cast over laurelled heads

So Be It

There are no rooms here
Better go right on
No light shows
This world is finished, done

Let the dark come

Let night strike
Let no stone be left unturned
Let it be over
The lie told too often

Truth itself is wounded

Let it
Be over and done with
Forever
Houses for grisly whores
Light to light funeral trains
Let it
Be over and written

Off, everybody's bad debt

The Everlasting Contenders

Of the beast. . . an angel
Creatures of the earth
It is good
Any who praise not grandly

O but they should

But they should
Death waits for everything that lives
Beast of the wood
Grim beast of the wood

Who praise not grandly

Should should
Heart weeps for all things
Here
And is greatly comforted
For heart is the angel
Of all
Who praise not grandly

But wish they could

111

What Splendid Birthdays

The ears of the forest
Twitch in the sun
Flies of cloud
Are shaken off so carefully

See, they alight again

In confident purity
And their wings seem to rest
Against the sky like
Candleflames painted on a cake

Deer in the sunglow

Green ears
Twitching sleepily in the warmth
Of
A peaceful summer's afternoon
Later . . . the herd stirs awake
Antlers purpling
And the first match

Touches the darkling candelabra

Always Another Viewpoint

You climb three "golden steps"
Past some friendly "lions"
And "the skeleton
Of a king!" The "lions"

Belong to a woman

Who's said to
Be a bit off. Actually she's
A fine person. I
Think more misunderstood than mad.

I live next door

In the
House with the dwarfpalm trees
Growing
Up through the roof.
Over beer she tells me
Stories about
When she was a

Queen. On rainy nights.

A Trueblue Gentleman

This gentleman the charming duck
Quack quack says he
My tail's on
Fire, but he's only kidding

You can tell that

By his grin
He's one big grin, from wobbly
Feet to wobbly tail
Quack quack he tells us

Tail's on fire again

Ah yes
This charming gentleman the duck
With
His quaint alarms and
Trick of walking like a
Drunken hat
Quack quack says he

There's your fried egg

Where Every Prospect

There will be no evil
No throat bared in
Scarlet agony here
But only the green grass

Waving beside peaceful roads

Along which gay
Runners carry thoughts of the sun
To fill the wilderness
With animals of loftier design

Than bowed to thug

And gun
In whose image created they
This
Where no peace is
Where only the stench of
Smoking flesh
Can adequately say, Now

Man is not evil

The Constant Bridegrooms

Far down the purple wood
Coats of a company
Of silent soldiers
Flap idly in the wind

There they have stood

Since early day
Faces turned incuriously to the sound
Of the dry rustling
Of leaves in the wind

No command has reached

Them there
All silent have they stood
As
Though they were asleep •
Now night darkens their coats
Far away
Their names are spoken
Somewhere at world's end

The Unreturning Hosts

Supreme in the distance, veiled
As one's own horizon,
The ancients stand,
Immutably shadowless in lengthening obliquity.

Stone is the rain

That falls on
Them. Panthers of frozen gold pad
Soundlessly round their shrouded
Immobility, while history's piping flutes

Shred hollowly against their

Stone music.
Honey-combed with shadow, great
Unsorrowing
Roses garland their sleep.
And stone is the air. . .
Of stone,
Their sea. . . *Dreamers lost*

In an unrotting solemnity.

Folly of Clowns

Come laughing when the wind
Has blown a hole
In the world
See the moving sparkle covers

Such chits as orchards

Thrones and caravansaries
Blackened eye-sockets above the **grit**
And silt of destinies
O come here laughing anyway

And let your head

Be daft
With sun and glitter of
Running
Naked beside the waters
As in pallid sand life's
Statues sleep
Tattered arm waves up!

School keep or not

All the Flowery

Along the red ledge I
Counted so many blossoms
That from first
To last nothing could hold

Them. No number of

Vases or even
Countries like Seyn or Merry Aden.
No number of horses
Black as inked snow with

The pink stains of

Girls on
Their massive backs could stride
Through
Even the first row.
And I, as my fathers
Would . . . watching
The nude sad riding

With joy, with fear

Lowellville Cemetery: Twilight

Gone silence down lowered sun
O at this each
Of everything here
These poor knotted hands lost

Under the darkened foam

Of grass. Stone
Unto stone and flesh unto flesh
Scattered as cold petals
On the floor of winter's

Own walking. All should

Be dark.
And dark on dark forever
Now.
Sundown and world, too.
As it is for them,
Lying here.
Why is it not?

Why is it not

Little Cannibal's Bedtimesong

2 bres's, 'n' 'gongo 'brella
Th' goddum buckwheat clovah
Sun he shimes
Birdz he sing-bes loudah loudah

4 she am mimbes

I'n like hur
Bettah'n even m' own fambly mothah
Oz sun he shimes
Birdz he sing-bes up top

Th' goddum buckwheat clovah

Me'n' hur
Dun't wunt no crocodilin' heah
Nohowah
'Lissa eat hur papah
I'n eat 2 each ob
M' couseens
No eat 'Lissa though

I'n no crazly barsted

Encounter at Nightfall

Smashed bones. Gristle of ribs.
Brittle thigh-cases agape.
Scoured. Racked. Gutted.
Bristling with crawling pocks. Grizzling

In the wart-kinked,

Gyring, pustulant light.
Brattle of shale on craggy tusks.
The gentle terrible faces
Clotted over, empty eye-sockets

Staring without much hope,

Or surprise.
What met they here as
Night
Fell? Did the sun
Go down weeping as they
Were slain?
Horror walk the earth?

Pity drain the sea?

122

In Order To

Apply for the position (I've forgotten now for what) I had to marry the Second Mayor's daughter by twelve noon. The order arrived three minutes of.

I already had a wife; the Second Mayor was childless: but I did it.

Next they told me to shave off my father's beard. All right. No matter that he'd been a eunuch, and had succumbed in early childhood: I did it, I shaved him.

Then they told me to burn a village; next, a fair-sized town; then, a city; a bigger city; a small, down-at-heels country; then one of "the great powers"; then another (another, another)—In fact, they went right on until they'd told me to burn up every man-made thing on the face of the earth! And I did it, I burned away every last trace, I left nothing, nothing of any kind whatever.

Then they told me to blow it all to hell and gone! And I blew it all to hell and gone (oh, didn't I). . .

Now, they said, put it back together again; put it all back the way it was when you started.

Well. . . it was my turn then to tell *them* something! Shucks, I didn't want any job that bad.

Soon It Will

Be showtime again. Somebody will paint beautiful faces all over the sky. Somebody will start bombarding us with really

123

wonderful letters. . . letters full of truth, and gentleness, and humility. . . Soon (it says here). . .

There Are Two

Ways about it. In fact, that only scratches the surface; for—well, had you seen the weeds, the weeds—even those weeds growing just below the outer edge of the wall! that would fix you! Crested. . . tubular. . . a few with—well, sort of hands. . .

In fact, I told my friend Flip, "Flip, you've got to do something about those weeds, especially those weeds down there just under the stains along the wall by the gate." But as usual he was monkeying around the car. It was almost dark by the time he got downstairs again, and the first thing he said was: "Do you want that other set of pipes inside, or do you want them curled around the hood?"

I told him curled around would be just dandy as a pair of little pink panties.

So. You know how it is. Sure, I had come there looking for that elusive oyster, happiness. Yep, that's what I was after, that goddam little sad-faced, buck-toothed oyster, happiness. And what had I got? Do I *really* have to tell you?

After a while I went out and climbed up on top of the wall. It had started to rain again. Pretty soon it was coming down in the large economy size buckets. I tore up all my identification papers and stripped down to where I had only one shoe and my hat on. Then I stood up on my hind legs and shouted:

"So! Enough's enough, you lousy, scrounging bastards! I'm off to join the Indians, see!" Then taking my other shoe off, I added: "And while you're about it, to hell with the Indians too, for that matter!"

Opening the Window

They called across to ask me to get some beer and come up and cut a few touches.

I'd already gone to bed but I got some clothes on and went down to the store for the beer and some of that nice dry kind of salami.

When I got up there were two old women and a tall skinny man sitting half dressed holding musical instruments.

By half dressed I mean the old women were in their birthday suits and the skinny fellow had a couple heavy overcoats on over his regular duds.

And speaking of musical instruments I refer to the fact that each of them was holding a full-blown mermaid in formfitting tights that was sort of crooning-like in a Greek accent.

As I commenced to set my parcels on the bed another old lady came barging out of the closet on zebraback.

After I lifted her off she said she had herself a sore behind from riding all the way up from Boston and would I mind holding her for a while. Pretty soon they wanted I should fetch some more beer and I found out the only way I could manage her up and down the narrow stairs was to go back-

125

wards and to squeeze like all hell on her long legs and even then those bony knees of hers sounded like somebody having a fit with a snaredrum on either side of us. And every trip I went to a different store and they kept getting farther and farther away. I took the next day off and moved into a YMCA.

It Takes Few Kinds

They made very little of such events—*Horses rising out of the water, the dark hair of the riders beautiful in the moonlight. . .*

Where one moment you would see nothing except the peaceful silvering of the water—*Great blond horses rising slowly into the sky, the dark and the beautiful hair of the riders trailing down. . . down. . .*

The dark and the beautiful hair trailing down through the moonlight—No, they made very little of such things.

One moment you would see only the water. . .

Then great icy blond horses would begin to rise slowly into the sky. . . And the dark and the beautiful hair of the maiden riders would trail down through the moonlight—But, actually, they made very little of things along that general line.

126

To Be Charmed

Seemed enough ambition for anyone with sense.

Scant matter with what. Be it only with the serenity of veils at the funeral of a river, or even with the compassion of first snow upon a blackened wood. (Of course taste did set certain limits: a bit of all too responsible soul-baiting went a long way to Redjellyhead Fair.)

Those horriblenesses of words that never, never, never, never, O never have anything at all to do with the lives of the people who say them, or to whom they are said. . . "Mercy." "Gentleness." "Peace." Mercy. . ! Gentleness. . ! *Peace.* . !

Moon "Continued"

Right after the Moon was got rid of, a moon was brought on. The same moon, of course, but a different Moon.

In what the "second" moon resembled that Moon of "the first instance" might extraordinarily have given some clue to their essential sameness, but this, alas, was only the usual deal and by then, certainly not surprisingly, the number and, well. . . "tone" of substitution had become somewhat involved, even, one might say, just a shade, only a shade, mind you, but still a shade, unfair.

Having said that, it remains only to say that I could not, this minute, give you any good reason why I should have expected them to be content with simple substitutions—you know, the "m"-moon, M-"Moon" sort of thing—but. . . I was hoping

. . . no, I was disappointed. . . yes, I was *disappointed*. . . I was bitterly disappointed, if you like, that they had to up and move on to another table and a new game just as I was beginning to catch the drift of some of the simpler plays.

The Great Sled-Makers

They get drunk, these Great Sled-Makers. Their copper mugs, around which their fingers easily circle once, and once again, hold what's called a "quart handsome" (about five and 3/8s gallons mirke-measure).

The Great Sled-Makers get drunk like other people do hopeless. An hour or two old they demand whiskey, and poor slaphoppy brute the mother who'd not lay them lovely on. . . all pink-fuzzy, ah, happy little belchers, rest ye well in between the worlds, as you might say.

Seven sees most married. Typically they live above saloons, their sole furniture a firehouse pole.

For, you must understand, it doesn't take a few hours or even a few days to make a Great-Sled; it takes closer to a thousand years.

Eleven have been built so far, not counting of course those which slip away from time to time (no doubt you've heard of tidal waves and earthquakes). Each is heavier than all the mountains placed together on a table having proper equipment for weighing of this sort; each requires a highway of at least a million lanes. . . at the very least. In other words, the Great-Sleds are not small. Just picture them! with their

128

runners of molten silver, their golden bodies painted a screaming red under a zigzag of yellow and buff stripes. The effect is quite nice. Only so far, you've probably guessed by now, nobody's bought nary a one.—*Whh-iskey, bo-oy!*

Not Many Kingdoms Left

I write the lips of the moon upon her shoulders. In a temple of silvery farawayness I guard her to rest.

For her bed I write a stillness over all the swans of the world. With the morning breath of the snow leopard I cover her against any hurt.

Using the pen of rivers and mountaintops I store her pillow with singing.

Upon her hair I write the looking of the heavens at early morning.

—Away from this kingdom, from this last undefiled place, I write civilizations, governments, and all other spirit-forsaken and soldiery institutions. O cold beautiful blossoms, the lips of the moon moving upon her shoulders. . . Stand off! *Stand off!*

Often Was It

Because, straying through the wine-gardens with the stainless impermanence of old poems spread out upon the wind like the ghostly sails of so many foundered ships. . .

And seeking through the silvery branches of the appletree for sandals that would suit the little walking feet of the moon. . .

Was it because, knowing what dye reddens the canvas of this earth now, and what howling substance covers these shoes. . .

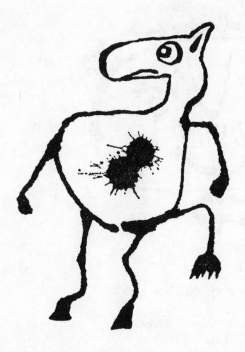

The Cowboy Who Went to College

There was a cowboy went to college,
Where somebody spilled ink on his horse.
He went to the dean in charge of such things
And was told that that gentleman
Had just popped out to the can again.
"Oh, he has, has he!" cried the cowboy;
"And me thinking it might be an accident—
"Why, hell, it's part of the damn curriculum!"

131

The Little Man with Wooden Hair

There was a little man with wooden hair
Who'd sneak into the rear of busses
And holler, "Somebody just ate my mother!"
For that way, of course, he could count on a quick trim
Without having to pay for the broken window.

The Tame Streetcar Conductor

There was a tame streetcar conductor
Who one day was considerably surprised
To have it suddenly bite his behind;
So next morning he reported for work
Disguised as a broad-minded chambermaid . .
And now lives with the company president's daughter.

The Careless Little Spy

There was a careless little spy
Who carried the Secret Code in the same briefcase
With the Master Plan and a wad of dancehall tickets;
Which may explain why some very Big Wheels
Are running about on their rims this morning.

The Forgetful Little Commuter

There was a forgetful little commuter
Who one morning boarded a large sheepish dog
And rode to a splashing stop beside a fireplug;
Arrived home, he hung up his snapbrim wife,
And briefly kissing his hat, said, "Those damn forecasters!
I suppose that cloudburst is their idea of fair weather!"

135

The Man Who Was Shorter Than Himself

There was a man two inches shorter than himself
Who always kept getting stuck in the sidewalk;
And when the curious townsmen came
To yank his arms and crush his hat,
He'd spit in the eye of the lean,
And steal the wallets off the fat.

136

The Little Man Who Saw a Grass

There was a little man who saw a grass
Kicking some beetles off the piano;
So he went to an old sage and demanded:
"Exactly whose chivalry does this defend?"
To which the old sage immediately responded:
"Quick! some water, bub—I smell beard-smoke!"

137

The Celery-Flute Player

There was a celery-flute player
Who got himself caught burning fire
On top of some old hoodlum's lake;
They wanted to hit him with a hammer,
But couldn't get up the admission
He would have charged them to see it.

138

I Went to the City

And there I did weep,
Men a-crowin' like asses,
And livin' like sheep.
Oh, can't hold the han' of my love!
Can't hold her little white han'!
Yes, I went to the city,
And there I did bitterly cry,
Men out of touch with the earth,
And with never a glance at the sky.
Oh, can't hold the han' of my love!
Can't hold her pure little han'!

139

One Who Hopes

Born like a veritable living prince
With small, pink, rectangular feet
And a disposition to hair, I stand
Under the blazing moon and wonder
At the disappearance of all holy things
From this once so promising world;
And it does not much displease me
To be told that at seven tomorrow morning
An Angel of Justice will appear,
And that he will clean up people's messes for them—
Because if he is, and he does, he'll be more apt
To rub their lousy snouts in it.

140

Only Cherries?

They didn't want me around
Said I couldn't have no cherries
Or watch them pick cherries
Or even stand near the table
Where one of those Kultur-Kookie-Klucks
With the big fat-legged smile
Was fixing to pop a nice red cherry
In on top of his gold spoon
You know I don't like those people
Who act as if a cherry
Was something they'd personally thought up

141

All the Roary Night

It's dark out, Jack
The stations out there don't identify themselves
We're in it raw-blind, like burned rats
It's running out
All around us
The footprints of the beast, one nobody has any notion of
The white and vacant eyes
Of something above there
Something that doesn't know we exist
I smell heartbreak up there, Jack
A heartbreak at the center of things—
And in which we don't figure at all

142

How Come?

You ain't my brother now
I don't trust the way
You stamp your feet on me
I don't shine up
To this devil-goosin' stuff
You been layin' on in my behalf
Oh you ain't my lovin' buddy now
Sometime I think the manner
You come in my house
And dirty-arm me around
Is something I don't particularly cherish

143

The Peaceful Lier

I used to flit about hoping
To brush up
On what everybody
Said was so special.
Well, I saw the big shtoonks
Kicking the cans off
The little shtoonks—*and!* . .
Charging them for the service.
Now, I admit that's a pretty special setup,
But if you don't mind I think
I'll just lie this one out in my own way.

144

And with the Sorrows of This Joyousness

O apple into ant and beard
Into barn, clock into cake and dust
Into dog, egg into elephant and fingers
Into fields, geese into gramophones and hills
Into houses, ice into isotopes and jugs
Into jaguars, kings into kindnesses and lanes
Into lattices, moons into meanwhiles and nears
Into nevers, orphans into otherwises and pegs
Into pillows, quarrels into quiets and races
Into rainbows, serpents into shores and thorns
Into thimbles, O unders into utmosts and vines
Into villages, webs into wholenesses and years
Into yieldings . . O zeals of these unspeaking
And forever unsayable zones!

145

New Directions Paperbooks

Prince Ilango Adigal, *Shilappadikaram:*
The Ankle Bracelet. NDP162.
Corrado Alvaro, *Revolt in Aspromonte.*
NDP119.
Chairil Anwar, *Selected Poems.* WPS2.
Djuna Barnes, *Nightwood.* NDP98.
Charles Baudelaire, *Flowers of Evil.*† NDP71.
Eric Bentley, *Bernard Shaw.* NDP59.
Jorge Luis Borges, *Labyrinths.* NDP186.
Alain Bosquet, *Selected Poems.*† WPS4.
Kay Boyle, *Thirty Stories.*
Breakthrough to Peace. (Anthology) NDP124.
William Bronk, *The World, the Worldless.*
(SFR) NDP157.
Buddha, *The Dhammapada.*
(Babbitt translation) NDP188.
Louis-Ferdinand Céline,
Journey to the End of the Night. NDP84.
Blaise Cendrars, *Selected Writings.*† NDP203.
Bankim-chandra Chatterjee,
Krishnakanta's Will. NDP120.
Jean Cocteau, *The Holy Terrors.* NDP212.
The Infernal Machine. NDP235.
Contemporary German Poetry.†
(Anthology) NDP148.
Gregory Corso,
Happy Birthday of Death. NDP86.
Long Live Man. NDP127.
Edward Dahlberg, *Because I Was Flesh.*
NDP227.
Edward Dahlberg Reader. NDP246.
David Daiches, *Virginia Woolf.*
(Revised) NDP96.
Robert Duncan, *Bending the Bow.* NDP255.
Richard Eberhart, *Selected Poems.* NDP198.
Russell Edson, *The Very Thing That Happens.*
NDP137.
William Empson,
Seven Types of Ambiguity. NDP204.
Some Versions of Pastoral. NDP92.
Lawrence Ferlinghetti,
A Coney Island of the Mind. NDP74.
Her. NDP88.
Routines. NDP187.
Starting from San Francisco. NDP220.
Unfair Arguments with Existence. NDP143.
Ronald Firbank, *Two Novels.* NDP128.
Dudley Fitts,
Poems from the Greek Anthology. NDP60.
F. Scott Fitzgerald, *The Crack-up.* NDP54.
Gustave Flaubert,
The Dictionary of Accepted Ideas. NDP230.
Sentimental Education. NDP63.
M. K. Gandhi, *Gandhi on Non-Violence.*
(ed. Thomas Merton) NDP197.
André Gide, *Dostoevsky.* NDP100.
Goethe, *Faust,* Part I.
(MacIntyre translation) NDP70.

Albert J. Guerard, *Thomas Hardy.* NDP185.
James B. Hall, *Us He Devours*
(SFR) NDP156.
Henry Hatfield, *Goethe.* NDP136.
Thomas Mann. (Revised Edition) NDP101.
John Hawkes, *The Cannibal.* NDP123.
The Lime Twig. NDP95.
Second Skin. NDP146.
The Beetle Leg. NDP239.
The Innocent Party. NDP238.
Hermann Hesse, *Siddhartha.* NDP65.
Edwin Honig, *García Lorca.* (Rev.) NDP102.
Christopher Isherwood, *The Berlin Stories.*
NDP134.
Henry James, *Stories of Writers and Artists.*
NDP57.
Alfred Jarry, *Ubu Roi.* NDP105.
James Joyce, *Stephen Hero.* NDP133.
Franz Kafka, *Amerika.* NDP117.
Bob Kaufman,
Solitudes Crowded with Loneliness. NDP199.
Hugh Kenner, *Wyndham Lewis.* NDP167.
Lincoln Kirstein,
Rhymes & More Rhymes of a Pfc. NDP202.
P. Lal, translator, *Great Sanskrit Plays.*
NDP142.
Tommaso Landolfi,
Gogol's Wife and Other Stories. NDP155.
Lautréamont, *Maldoror.* NDP207.
Denise Levertov, *O Taste and See.* NDP149.
The Jacob's Ladder. NDP112.
The Sorrow Dance. NDP222.
With Eyes at the Back of Our Heads.
NDP229.
Harry Levin, *James Joyce.* NDP87.
García Lorca, *Selected Poems.*† NDP114.
Three Tragedies. NDP52.
Five Plays. NDP232.
Carson McCullers, *The Member of the*
Wedding. (Playscript) NDP153.
Thomas Merton,
Cables to the Ace. NDP252.
Clement of Alexandria. Gift Edition.
NDP173.
Emblems of a Season of Fury. NDP140.
Original Child Bomb. NDP174.
Raids on the Unspeakable. NDP213.
Selected Poems. NDP85.
Henry Miller,
Big Sur & Oranges of Hieronymus Bosch.
NDP161.
The Colossus of Maroussi. NDP75.
The Cosmological Eye. NDP109.
Henry Miller on Writing. NDP151.
Remember to Remember. NDP111.
The Smile at the Foot of the Ladder.
NDP176.

Henry Miller,
Stand Still Like the Humming Bird.
NDP236.
The Time of the Assassins. NDP115.
The Wisdom of the Heart. NDP94.
Yukio Mishima, *Confessions of a Mask.*
NDP253.
Death in Midsummer. NDP215.
Eugenio Montale, *Selected Poems.*† NDP193.
Vladimir Nabokov, *Nikolai Gogol.* NDP78.
New Directions 17. (Anthology) NDP103.
New Directions 18. (Anthology) NDP163.
New Directions 19. (Anthology) NDP124.
New Directions 20. (Anthology) NDP248.
Charles Olson, *Selected Writings.* NDP231.
George Oppen,
Of Being Numerous. NDP245.
The Materials. (SFR) NDP122.
This In Which. (SFR) NDP201.
Wilfred Owen, *Collected Poems.* NDP210.
Nicanor Parra,
Poems and Antipoems.† NDP242.
Boris Pasternak, *Safe Conduct.* NDP77.
Kenneth Patchen, *Because It Is.* NDP83.
Doubleheader. NDP211.
Hallelujah Anyway. NDP219.
The Journal of Albion Moonlight. NDP99.
Memoirs of a Shy Pornographer. NDP205.
Selected Poems. NDP160.
Plays for a New Theater. (Anthology)
NDP216.
Ezra Pound, *ABC of Reading.* NDP89.
Classic Noh Theatre of Japan. NDP79.
The Confucian Odes. NDP81.
Confucius to Cummings. (Anthology)
NDP126.
Guide to Kulchur. NDP257.
Literary Essays. NDP250.
Love Poems of Ancient Egypt. Gift Edition.
NDP178.
Selected Poems. NDP66.
Translations.† (Enlarged Edition) NDP145.
Philip Rahv, *Image and Idea.* NDP67.
Carl Rakosi, *Amulet.* NDP234.
Raja Rao, *Kanthapura.* NDP224.
Herbert Read, *The Green Child.* NDP208.
Jesse Reichek, *Etcetera.* NDP196.
Kenneth Rexroth, *Assays.* NDP113.
Collected Shorter Poems. NDP243.
100 Poems from the Chinese. NDP192.
100 Poems from the Japanese.† NDP147.

Charles Reznikoff,
By the Waters of Manhattan. (SFR)
NDP121.
Testimony: The United States 1885–1890.
(SFR) NDP200.
Arthur Rimbaud, *Illuminations.*† NDP56.
Season in Hell & Drunken Boat.† NDP97.
Jean-Paul Sartre, *Baudelaire.* NDP233.
Nausea. NDP82.
Delmore Schwartz, *Selected Poems.*
NDP241
Stevie Smith, *Selected Poems.* NDP159.
Gary Snyder, *The Back Country.* NDP249.
Enid Starkie, *Arthur Rimbaud,* NDP254.
Stendhal, *Lucien Leuwen.*
Book I: *The Green Huntsman.* NDP107.
Book II: *The Telegraph.* NDP108.
Jules Supervielle, *Selected Writings.*† NDP209.
Dylan Thomas, *Adventures in the Skin Trade.*
NDP183.
A Child's Christmas in Wales. Gift Edition.
NDP181.
Portrait of the Artist as a Young Dog.
NDP51.
Quite Early One Morning. NDP90.
Under Milk Wood. NDP73.
Lionel Trilling, *E. M. Forster.* NDP189.
Martin Turnell, *The Art of French Fiction.*
NDP251.
Paul Valéry, *Selected Writings.*† NDP184.
Vernon Watkins, *Selected Poems.* NDP221.
Nathanael West, *Miss Lonelyhearts &*
Day of the Locust. NDP125.
George F. Whicher, tr.,
The Goliard Poets.† NDP206.
John Willett, *The Theatre of Bertolt Brecht.*
NDP244.
Tennessee Williams,
The Glass Menagerie. NDP218.
Hard Candy. NDP225.
In the Winter of Cities. NDP154.
27 Wagons Full of Cotton. NDP217.
One Arm & Other Stories. NDP237.
William Carlos Williams,
The Autobiography. NDP223.
The Farmers' Daughters. NDP106.
In the American Grain. NDP53.
In the Money. NDP240.
Many Loves. NDP191.
Paterson. Complete. NDP152.
Pictures from Brueghel. NDP118.
Selected Poems. NDP131.
White Mule. NDP226.

(SFR) A New Directions / San Francisco Review Book.   † Bilingual.

**Complete descriptive catalog available free on request from
New Directions, 333 Sixth Avenue, New York 10014.**